JENNIFER SERRAVALLO

FOREWORD BY Debbie Miller

The
Literacy Teacher's
Playbook

GRADES K–2

Four Steps for Turning Assessment Data
into Goal-Directed Instruction

HEINEMANN
Portsmouth, NH

Heinemann
361 Hanover Street
Portsmouth, NH 03801–3912
www.heinemann.com

Offices and agents throughout the world

The author and publisher wish to thank those who have generously given permission to reprint borrowed material:

Excerpts from the Common Core State Standards © Copyright 2010. National Governors Association Center for Best Practices and Council of Chief State School Officers. All rights reserved.

Figure 1.9: "Running-Record Note-Taking" from *Conferring with Readers: Supporting Each Student's Growth and Independence* by Jennifer Serravallo and Gravity Goldberg. Copyright © 2007 by Jennifer Serravallo and Gravity Goldberg. Published by Heinemann, Portsmouth, NH. All rights reserved.

Credits continue on page iv.

Library of Congress Cataloging-in-Publication Data
Serravallo, Jennifer.
    The literacy teacher's playbook, grades K–2 : four steps for turning assessment data into goal-directed instruction / Jennifer Serravallo ; foreword by Debbie Miller.
        pages cm
    Includes bibliographical references.
    ISBN: 978-0-325-05300-4
    1. Language arts (Elementary)—United States—Evaluation.   I. Title.
LB1576.S343424 2014
372.6'049—dc23   2013040938

Editor: Zoë Ryder White
Production: Victoria Merecki
Typesetter: Gina Poirier, Gina Poirier Design
Cover and interior designs: Suzanne Heiser
Cover and interior photographs: Michelle Baker and Nick Christoff
Manufacturing: Steve Bernier

Printed in the United States of America on acid-free paper
18 17 16 PAH 3 4 5

For Lola and Vivie

Credits continued from page ii:

Figure 1.10: "A Tough Day for Thomas" by Shannon Rigney Keane from The Reading and Writing Project © 2010: http://readingandwritingproject.com/public/themes/rwproject/resources /assessments/additional_tools/tough_day_for_thomas.pdf. Reprinted by permission of Teachers College Reading and Writing Project, Columbia University, New York.

Figures 1.11 and A.2: Student Response forms from *Independent Reading Assessment: Fiction* and *Independent Reading Assessment: Nonfiction* by Jennifer Serravallo. Copyright © 2012 and 2013 by Jennifer Serravallo. Published by Scholastic Inc. Reprinted by permission of the publisher.

Figure 2.8: Excerpt from *The Teeny Tiny Woman* by Jane O'Connor. Text copyright © 1986 by Random House. Illustrations by R.W. Alley, copyright © 1986 by R.W. Alley. Reprinted by permission of Random House Children's Books, a division of Random House LLC. All rights reserved.

Figures 2.9–2.16: Student expectations graphics from *Independent Reading Assessment: Fiction* and *Independent Reading Assessment: Nonfiction* by Jennifer Serravallo. Copyright © 2012 and 2013 by Jennifer Serravallo. Published by Scholastic Inc. Reprinted by permission of the publisher.

Figure 2.17: NAEP fluency scale (2002): https://nces.ed.gov/nationsreportcard/studies/ors /scale.asp. Reprinted by permission of the National Center for Education Statistics, Institute for Education Sciences, U.S. Department of Education.

Figure 4.3: "Three Levels of Decision Making to Move Children Toward Independence" from *Teaching Reading in Small Groups: Differentiated Instruction for Building Strategic, Independent Readers* by Jennifer Serravallo. Copyright © 2010 by Jennifer Serravallo. Published by Heinemann, Portsmouth, NH. All rights reserved.

Figure 4.4: Diagram of gradual release of responsibility from *Better Learning Through Structured Teaching: A Framework for the Gradual Release of Responsibility* by Douglas Fisher and Nancy Frey. Copyright © 2008 by the Association for Supervision and Curriculum Development (ASCD). Reprinted by permission of the Copyright Clearance Center on behalf of ASCD.

Figure 4.8: Class Profile form from *Independent Reading Assessment: Fiction* by Jennifer Serravallo. Copyright © 2012 by Jennifer Serravallo. Published by Scholastic Inc. Reprinted by permission of the publisher.

Figure 4.9: Planning Your Week form from *Independent Reading Assessment: Fiction* by Jennifer Serravallo. Copyright © 2012 by Jennifer Serravallo. Published by Scholastic Inc. Reprinted by permission of the publisher.

Contents

To download the student writing samples
and reproducible forms featured
throughout this book, please visit
www.heinemann.com/products/E05300.aspx
(click on the Companion Resources tab).

Foreword

Jen Serravallo and I have been friends for a while, even though we've never met. But by reading her earlier books, following her on Twitter, and reading her blog, I *feel* I know her. Now, after reading the page proof of *The Literacy Teacher's Playbook, Grades K–2*, I just *have* to meet her in person. And give her a hug.

My new favorite quote is from her blog entry of 12/19/13, which is headed "A Close Reading of Kids: Teaching Reading Like a Scientist":

> *I approach my teaching with a spirit of wonder and amazement. I ask questions that guide studies of inquiry about students specifically and about reading skills and processes in general. I collect information and puzzle over it, rearrange it, analyze it, and draw conclusions from it. And just when it might seem I'm done, I start the whole thing all over again—there is always more to think about, question, and learn.*

This is the spirit in which this book is written—studying kids closely and making smart decisions about where they are now and where they need to go. I'll admit the thought of all those assessment data made me apprehensive. Was this book going to be only about numbers and percentages? I needn't have worried. As Jen says up front, "This book is about being empowered by assessment, not being bogged down by it."

What I love most about this book is that Jen encourages us to expand our vision of what assessment is and what it can do for our teaching. Thoughtfully considering the authentic work children do every day produces real-time data we can use to plan and make wise decisions for individual, small-group, and whole-class instruction. Studied closely and used collectively these kinds of data—one child's saying to another, "I'm going to read my new book three times every day until I can read all the words"; a child's recording his questions on sticky notes to prepare for his book club; a child's using pictures or pictures and words to demonstrate her understanding of a book's big ideas—elevate student achievement and help ensure no child falls through the cracks.

Knowledge is power. This book shows you how to get to know—really know—every child in your care and teach in intentional, authentic, powerful ways. I encourage you to take advantage of Jen's expertise as she makes her four-step method visible and accessible through her interactions with two very different (and adorable!) learners, Emre and Marelle. Learn alongside Jen as she masterfully analyzes and interprets these students' actions, comments, questions, and work products; sets goals; creates action plans based on what they already know; and figures out where they need to go next. With Jennifer as your coach, you'll be inspired and motivated—perhaps even obligated—to get to know all your children as well as you know Emre and Marelle.

Every day you stay with this in-depth inquiry and analysis, you'll be smarter about your kids and what they need. Give yourself time and be patient—the hard work you're doing is going to make a difference in the lives of the children you teach. And yours, too. Happy reading! (And if you see Jennifer Serravallo before I do, please pass along that hug from me for writing such a thoughtful and timely book!)

Debbie Miller

Acknowledgments

Gone are the days when teachers would walk into their classroom, close the door, and go about their business. The work it takes to become a great teacher is in large part teamwork. And so it is with me, a teacher turned staff developer turned author. Everything has been possible only because of the great teams who support me.

Thanks, first, to the team at the Teachers College Reading and Writing Project (TCRWP). Much of the work described in this book began when I was a senior staff developer at this amazing organization. Thanks especially to the founding director, Lucy Calkins, and senior staff members Kathleen Tolan, Mary Ehrenworth, Amanda Hartman, and Laurie Pessah for your inspiration, encouragement, leadership, knowledge, and generosity. Every member of TCRWP, past and present, has influenced me in immeasurable ways; every Thursday for eight years we met to ask good questions, outgrow our best thinking, and support one another in our own professional development. Specifically, I want to thank Carl Anderson, Mary Chiarella, Donna Santman, Colleen Cruz, Cory Gillette, Brooke Geller, Emily Smith, Elizabeth Moore, Ami Mehta, Joe Yukish, and Alison Porcelli. Your footprints are all over this book.

Thanks as well to the teams of educators with whom I've been lucky enough to learn beside. I have been refining the ideas in this book based on feedback from brilliant teachers at Public Schools 59, 63, 158, and 277, in New York City; teachers in Bexley, Ohio; Philadelphia, Pennsylvania; and Chappaqua, New York; teachers enrolled in TCRWP summer institutes; and teachers in my specialty courses and leadership groups. All that time you thought I was teaching you, I was learning from you!

Thanks to Trixie Della Rosa and Polly Luckett for your endless support and wise counsel. Everyone needs people in their professional lives whom they trust completely and can rely on. I'm lucky to have you both.

Thank you to the team members at Heinemann who have helped to make this book possible. Thanks to Kate Montgomery for seeing promise in the initial proposal and for matching me with the wonderful Zoë Ryder White who helped me turn the initial idea into two books, and so much more. Zoë, I am grateful for your critical questions, invaluable feedback, and enthusiasm. Thanks also to Patty Adams and Victoria Merecki, in production, and Eric Chalek, in marketing, for your creativity, time, and dedication.

Thank you to the team who helped make this book beautiful. Thanks to Joyce Boley, Danielle Dininno, Karyn Grant, Jessica Figueroa, and Kristin Bubnis at Bowne-Munro

Elementary School for hosting us for two days and spending so much time sprucing up your classrooms before you packed it all up at the end of the year. Thanks to Nick Christoff and Michelle Baker for taking the photographs and to Suzanne Heiser for your beautiful cover design and for making the interior of the book easy to read and navigate.

This book would not be possible without FJ DeRobertis who invited me into his classroom to observe his students, photocopied student work samples that have become part of the fabric of this book, and offered his thoughts about his students along the way. Thanks also to Kristine Mraz for lending some last-minute kindergarten work samples.

And finally, thank you to my family. To Jen, Lola, and Vivian: thank you for helping me laugh and always being there to balance all my seriousness. Lola and Vivie, one of my greatest hopes for you is that you find a career you love as much I love mine. Still, it's never easy to turn from you to the computer or leave the house at the crack of dawn to make my way to a school or airport or conference. Thank you for understanding.

Introduction

June planning was a tradition in my school. The classrooms in our non–air-conditioned New York City public school were stifling with humidity, and the children wilted like flowers on their desks. As hard as it was to leave them for a whole day knowing we'd soon be saying good-bye for the summer, my colleagues and I would spend the day in a small conference room adjacent to the principal's office.

We'd start by planning the scope and sequence for the year. What units would we tackle in reading? In writing? How would literacy work align with our social studies goals? We'd reference the standards (at that time, they were the state standards) to make sure we were hitting everything across the year. Then we'd dive into the nitty-gritty of the first month. We'd plan each lesson carefully, being sure to spiral and alternate skills. We'd craft our minilesson teaching points, ensuring they were clear, yet rigorous. We'd choose our mentor texts and our read-alouds, and we'd begin marking up the pages where we'd think aloud and where we'd have the kids turn and talk.

We left the room so proud by the end of that day, with a clear road map of the year to come. But if I knew then what I know now, I'd have sent myself back to the drawing board.

All of that curriculum planning was completely devoid of the students in front of me.

I'd like to say this was a mistake I made only in my first year teaching, but I actually repeated it time and again. Whether teaching social studies, science, reading, writing, or math—I didn't quite understand as I now do the difference between teaching a class of children and teaching curriculum and to the standards.

Some years, I reluctantly admit, I had groups of students who made very little progress. I could never quite put my finger on why this was. I didn't understand the difference between assessing students to check up on understandings and assessing students to form my teaching plan. It's the difference between giving your students a spelling test on Friday to see if they can spell the words *man*, *can*, *pen*, and *ten* and giving students a spelling inventory to learn if they know how to spell with initial consonants or understand how to spell C-V-C words in general, and, if not, working with students to learn about short vowels.

My I-wish-I-knew-then-what-I-know-now experiences are the main inspiration for this book. I wanted to write a book to help you to really *see* your students so that all of your planning for students as individuals, groups, and a whole class is based in what kids already know, understand, and are able to do. I wanted to help ensure that the teaching we choose to do aims high enough and helps move kids to the next step.

This book isn't necessarily going to help you plan the specifics of your next unit of study on tackling tricky words, or writing poetry. What it will do, though, is help you understand your students with a kind of depth that will allow you to tweak the reading and writing units you plan to teach to ensure you're meeting the needs of your students and to ensure that you're giving each of them opportunities for success.

This book is about being empowered by data and assessment, not bogged down by it. It's about getting to know each and every student in your classroom well and feeling confident in your decision making because of your reliance on assessments. It's about reclaiming and reinvigorating the term *classroom-based assessment* for the current era, when it's all the more critical that teachers know how to analyze the work students do each day, in groups and individually. Because if teachers don't have their fingers on the pulse of students' response to instruction, who does?

If you are reading both this book and *The Literacy Teacher's Playbook, Grades 3–6* (Serravallo 2014), you're going to notice some similarities and some differences. The overarching structure of the books is the same, because on a macro level I'm hoping you'll take away from this book an understanding of a process you can employ to study student work, establish goals, and begin consistent goal-directed instruction across grade levels. Much of the content, however, is different. Because so much of your success with the process described in this book depends upon how much you know about the teaching of reading and writing, I've included lots of specific information about what types of student work to collect, what to look for in that student work, and what types of goals are age-appropriate. Of course, K–2 and 3–6 are still wide spans, and a 200-page book can't explore everything there is to know about reading and writing at every stage, but throughout both books I will direct you to resources and materials that will further support your grade-level-specific knowledge.

The four chapters in this book illuminate a four-step protocol, or procedure, you may use. Across these four chapters, you'll learn how to collect data that are helpful, analyze the data correctly, and make plans based on that data. You'll learn how to lead conversations with individual students to establish goals that will focus your work together, and their work independently, during your literacy time. You'll learn ways to manage these individual goals to help your reading and writing class hum with productivity and intention, which will have big payoffs for students. The four steps are:

This book is about being empowered by data and assessment, not bogged down by it.

- Step 1: Collect data.
- Step 2: Analyze data.
- Step 3: Interpret data and establish a goal.
- Step 4: Create an action plan.

These four steps will function like a playbook: the indispensible guide a football coach relies on to know just what to do in certain situations.

Chapter 1 details step 1: collecting data. Football coaches prepare for Sunday afternoon's game by collecting films of the opposing team's past games. They send out scouts to watch the other team play against different types of teams in different types of weather, at different times of day. As teachers, we need to collect information from a variety of situations— both reading and writing—that highlight different aspects of a student. We'll look at five lenses for reading (engagement, fluency, print work, comprehension, and conversation) as well as qualities of good writing, writing process, and writing engagement. I'm going to offer suggestions on what the data might look like that will give you insight about each of these lenses, a rationale for why you'd want to collect it, and quick instructions on how to collect it.

Chapter 2 gives information on step 2: analyzing data. Once coaches have all their data—their films and notes from the assistant scouts—they sit down and analyze it. Looking at which players are strongest in which situations and what plays the team tends to have the most success with helps them get ready to make a plan. Of course, when looking at these data, football coaches have a great deal of content knowledge about what it takes to be successful. In Chapter 2, I offer you, the literacy teacher, the content you need to look closely at each piece of data and analyze it. Through the analysis, I'll guide you in noticing individual student strengths as well as opportunities for next steps.

In Chapter 3, we'll explore step 3: interpreting data and crafting a goal. From their analysis of the opposing team and their individual players' tendencies, coaches make generalizations about the types of plays that will have the biggest payoff in the upcoming game. They establish goals for how to deal with each situation. As literacy teachers, we go about the work of looking for patterns and trends across the data you've analyzed to come up with some interpretations, or theories, about what's going on with the student and what goals might have the biggest payoff.

The fourth and final chapter elaborates on step 4: developing an action plan. It's game time. Based on all the analysis and planning, coaches need to know what plays will help bring success to their team. For the students in your class, I'll show you how to take the established goal and make a plan, both short and long term. We'll consider how to follow up with ongoing assessment and track progress over time.

I wrote this book as if I were planning a workshop. Its structure is rooted in the balanced literacy, "I do, we do, you do" framework. Throughout the book, you'll learn *from me* and then *with me*. I'll act like your coach, so you can be a coach for your students.

I do: I'm going to model my process by sharing what I'm thinking during each step and offering a lot of content support as well. I've chosen one "case study" child, a first grader named Marelle, whom you'll get to know well across the course of the book through all of her work samples. You'll be able to study her work and read along as I voice over my analysis of her work. You'll read my conclusions about her in the tables provided throughout the chapters.

We do: I've enclosed work samples from a second student, Emre, also a first grader. Here's your chance to try what I'm writing about with a little support from me. I'm going to include some of my own thoughts about Emre's work in Appendix A. You can study his work alone or with a colleague—although I recommend the latter. Just as a head coach depends on the advice and thinking from his offensive and defensive coordinators, your insights about the student(s) you've chosen will be greatest with many minds on the task. Emre's work can be printed from www.heinemann.com/products/E05300.aspx (click on the Companion Resources tab), spread out on the table, and passed around if you're working with colleagues. You might use work from one of your own students during this phase instead of, or in addition to, using his work.

If you follow along with these two students I've chosen—Marelle and Emre—you'll notice they are very different. Emre is the type of student who seems to have it all down—

the child you might leave alone because you can't figure out what to do to challenge him further. Marelle will seem quite different. She's the type of student whose immediate needs are more visible, a student that teachers often strive to understand better. She's a student that might be the type identified to be in need of intervention support. Both of these students are the types of children I get asked about most often: the types of students teachers feel they most want support in trying to understand better.

You do: My hope is that after you've seen the model (Marelle) and had some guided practice (Emre), you'll be ready to try out the process independently with your own students.

Throughout Chapters 1 and 2, I've included references to some of those authors whose work in the teaching of reading and writing has influenced me most significantly. I include these references because I hope that as you work through the protocol to develop a goal for your chosen student(s), you also discover a professional learning goal for yourself—and seek out some of the sources I mention to begin your own self-study.

Finally, I hope that by going through this process you'll be all the more attuned to ways that real, authentic student work contains some of the most powerful information we have to make positive differences in our students' literacy.

Ready, set, hike!

Chapter 1

Collecting Data

ASSESSMENT LENSES AND TOOLS

When children in New York City turn three and four, some parents begin to panic. You see, when students turn four, they may take a standardized test to determine if they will earn a seat in one of the city's "gifted and talented" kindergarten classrooms. The validity of these tests has long been questioned—whether a child succeeds with this test at age four has more to do with factors such as socioeconomic status and parental education level than it does with actual IQ, or even whether or not they'd still be considered "gifted" several years later. Still, administrators in a large urban district crave data, and many parents with means even send their tiny children to special tutors to help them get ready for these exams. Administrators want the numbers, the percentiles, and the stanine scores. This, they feel, will help them have confidence when they make decisions for these very young children.

Over the last few years we have seen an effort to quantify everything in schools. "Accountability" is the name of the game. Teachers have spoken up and argued back about the validity and reliability of testing our youngest children. I'd agree, and yet,

1

I'd add that the data themselves are not the problem. I am the daughter of an analytical chemist. I *like data*. (There, I said it.) But when I think of the words *data* and *school* together, I think of *real student work* that will help teachers teach.

To me, data are not only the numbers and letters, but also the actual stuff that a student produces. It's students' everyday work. With this book, I hope to begin to shift your thinking about what *data* means and help you to see that much of what you can pull out of your students' messy seat pocket is actually data. Kindergarteners' first invented spellings are data. Running records are data. Transcripts of student conversations are data. A child's drawings representing a story are data. All of these are; that is, if you treat them as such. If you don't *use* them, they may start to feel like unnecessary paperwork for both you and your students.

This chapter is the first step in a four-part protocol to help you know your students and make purposeful evidence-based decisions for cross-curricular reading and writing instruction.

• Step 1: Collect data.

- Step 2: Analyze data.
- Step 3: Interpret data and establish a goal.
- Step 4: Create an action plan.

In this chapter, you'll read about a handful of assessment lenses for reading and writing, and the examples of types of student work that will help you see your students through those lenses. I'll show you some examples and I'll encourage you to start collecting from your own classroom, right away. If you don't have artifacts like the ones I recommend at-the-ready, you might begin thinking about some lessons you can do or some time you can set aside for students to do the work.

Lenses and Tools for Assessing Reading and Writing

I recommend organizing reading assessments into five lenses that teachers might use to get to know readers. My purpose in organizing assessments into these five lenses is to help you to look through a lens that may be most familiar first, and then to offer assessment lenses that offer new ways of teaching reading that you may want to explore (Serravallo 2010).

The five lenses I recommend using when assessing readers are:

- reading engagement
- reading fluency
- print work/decoding
- reading comprehension
- conversation

On the next page, you'll also read about tools to study the skills and behaviors of emergent readers.

In this book, I won't stop with reading; I've also chosen to include writing. Reading and writing connections are important in assessment and instruction. When you notice similar strengths and needs in reading and writing, it gives you a way to make the most of the goal you provide for your student by repeating that work across parts of the child's day. When you notice an imbalance, you can use the stronger of the two to bolster that area in need of strengthening. This works as well for even the youngest children who may come to school recognizing just a few of their letters and writing with loops and pictures.

The lenses we can use when assessing writers are:

- writing engagement
- qualities of good writing

In the discussion of each lens, I offer options of tools to use to assess with that lens in mind. You'll also find assessment ideas, or tools. However, I want to emphasize from the get-go that you get the clearest sense of a student if you use them all. Seeing a student in light of only one or two lenses limits both you and the student. It may cause you to make assumptions about a child that are untrue or choose to focus on something less important.

For example, if you only have a spelling inventory for first-grader Nick, you may know some things about his ability to encode. But without a complementary example as he reads, you could incorrectly assume what level books would be a best fit for him when it comes to decoding, and you'd have no information about what meaning he's making from those books. For that, you'd need to listen to him talk about his books, to jot some thoughts about his reading, and/or to talk to him after reading a book. Therefore, my recommended action in this section is that you try to collect *at least one* student artifact from each of the following lenses.

Early Kindergarten Lenses and Tools

Most of the examples of lenses and tools you'll find described and shown in detail within this book will be helpful for teachers of students who are reading conventionally (at least at level A/B). For emergent readers, which will be many students during the first few months of kindergarten, you'll also want to collect important information described by Clay (2013) in *An Observation Survey of Early Literacy Achievement*, McGill-Franzen (2006) in *Kindergarten Literacy*, and information from Sulzby's (1994) work on emergent reading behaviors and categories. Collecting and examining these types of artifacts is a huge part of getting to know children and planning the instruction at the start of the year. What you learn from these assessments will inform how you plan your whole-class, small-group, and individual teaching. This information includes:

- **Letter and letter-sound identification.** You'll show students all letters of the alphabet out of order, and ask students to tell you the name of the letter and the sound the letter makes. You'll record which letters and sounds the student knows and still needs to learn.

- **Emergent reading category.** You'll ask a child to "read" a story to you that you've read to that child many times. Stories with a conventional story structure such as *Harry the Dirty Dog* (Zion 2006), *Caps for Sale* (Slobodkina 1968), and *Corduroy* (Freeman 1976) work best. Although the child will not yet be reading the words, you'll make note of what the child does. Those in the earliest stages will point to pictures and label or comment on what is in the picture. Those in later stages will describe the actions on each page and will have a sense of beginning, middle, and end. As students progress, they will be able to sound like they are reading—giving lots of detail including what characters say and what the narrators say. A summary of Elizabeth Sulzby's categories for reading and corresponding categories for writing (1994) can be found in Appendix D.

- **Concepts about print.** You'll give a child a leveled book (around level D will work well) and you'll ask a series of questions to learn what the student understands about how books, and print, works. For example, "Where is the cover? Where is the back? Where do I start reading? Show me a letter. Show me a word. What is this (pointing to a period)?"

Assessing Reading Engagement

When we consider a student's level of engagement, we are in essence assessing whether the child reads for pleasure or reads merely for school. *Engagement* refers to a reader's motivation and desire to read and her ability to read for sustained amounts of time.

It's no accident that I list this as the first lens. Research has proven time and again that for students to improve, they must read for long stretches of time, with just-right material, enjoying their texts (Allington 2011; Guthrie and Wigfield 1997; Calkins 2000; Serravallo 2010).

You and your students may already have a number of artifacts you can examine with an eye to assessing engagement. One possible tool for this is the **book log** (see Figures 1.1–1.3).

Depending on the student's reading level, the book log may include different amounts of and types of information. This is mainly because at lower levels (A–I) students will often reread a book many times, and by the time students are reading chapter books, they may reread a book just once or not at all. We want to be sure that the amount of writing students do to record their reading does not interfere significantly with the actual reading.

Book Titles	Tally Marks
mr. Putter and tabby feed the fish	
Poler Bear cub	J
Fins wings and legs	
wake up Black Bear	
Pandr Bear cud	l
the 100 Day of scHool	ʌ
its sPring	ʰʰ
robert and the rocket	l l l l
my Brother Ant	ʰʰ
GEOrGE SHrinKs	l

Name: Mickey   Week of: 3-7

Figure 1.1 This simple tally log records the number of times a book has been read from start to finish. For this log to work, a child needs to know how to keep a tally. I often teach students to keep the log on their desks as they read and to record a tally mark on the log as soon as they finish one book. That completed book then goes into a "done" pile. An alternative way of doing this is to place a sticky note on the back cover of each of the dozen or so books in the student's baggie, and teach the student to tally on the sticky as soon as he or she closes the book.

It would take a child reading a book at level B longer to write the title than to read the entire book! For this reason, tally-type logs are often more appropriate for those at lower levels where books are shorter and rereading is more common.

Some kindergarten teachers I work with use rereading logs as early as October when children are rereading emergent storybooks. Many kindergarten teachers wait until mid-year when students are reading conventionally in B-, C-, and D-level books to introduce rereading logs that are aligned to the expected behaviors a reader might exhibit at that level. First-grade teachers and second-grade teachers typically decide to have everyone in the class logging their reading but choose a type for each student given the reading level of the student using it. You'll want to consider if the log is a tool to help you monitor engagement or if it becomes a distractor for the young children you teach. Obviously, the goal is engaged reading! So, if you've taught students how to use the log and it isn't working to help you, you will likely choose to discontinue its use.

Figure 1.2 This type of log is great to collect information about how many books have been read, which books have been read many times, and which books have been read few times. The teacher would first need to introduce purposes for rereading (i.e., to understand, to make a mind movie, to practice retelling, etc.). The student marks an "S" after each book has been read in school and an "H" when a title has been read at home. This student has read four books once each in school. By the end of the week, the teacher and student could reflect on what books were favorites, and could check in on the reading work the student has practiced independently.

Figure 1.3 Students use book logs to record texts' titles, the time they spend reading, and number of pages read. Depending on the age and writing ability of the student, you can have the child record start and end times and start and end pages or you can simply tell the child the number of minutes they've been reading. You can ask students to record a start page at the beginning of reading time and an end page at the end of reading time, or you can do as Kristine's teacher has done and ask the student just to indicate the chapters read.

Book logs are useful not only as records of what types of books students have read, but also to look for revealing patterns about students' engagement. Where are students and what are they reading when they are reading the most pages, for the longest time? Where are they and what are they reading when they are reading just a few pages, or for a very short time?

Name: Kristine	2nd Grade Book Log	Week of: 1/5	
Date	**Title**	**Start Time**	**End Time**
1/3	The Mitten.	6:20	6:40
1/4	Strega Nona.	7:00	7:25
1/5	Arthur Goes to Camp.	7:30	7:50
1/6	Boundless Grace.	4:00	4:25
1/7	The three sillies.	7:00	7:40
1/8	The Littles go exploring. Chapter 1,2,3,4	7:15	7:45
1/9	Chapter 5,6,7.	11:00	11:35
1/10	Chapter 8,9,10	10:00	10:30
1/12	Ch. 11,12,13,14.	11:00	11:30

Reading interest inventories (see Figure 1.4) are surveys that students can complete by writing their answers to questions independently, or by answering those questions orally during a conference. Student answers can offer insights about attitudes toward reading and their interests in general (which may help you to find books for them that will be engaging). For example, I might ask, "What do you do after school?" or "What TV shows do you watch?" Especially for students who are more reluctant readers, but really for all students, these sorts of questions help me match them to engaging books that they might not be aware of. For example, if there is a student who loves funny things but tells me she hates reading, I might suggest the Fly Guy series by Tedd Arnold, books by David Shannon like *No, David!* (1998) or maybe even Dr. Seuss.

Some students may be "teacher pleasers" who try to intuit what it is you're looking for. These students may not answer the questionnaire honestly, or may write answers that they think you want to hear. Asking questions in an open-ended fashion might help to ameliorate this problem. For example, instead of asking, "What's your favorite book?" you might say, "Are there any books you like?" The subtle difference between these two questions is a lack of assumption. Kids know that teachers want them to read, but sometimes finding out that reading hasn't been great for them so far can be an entry into an honest discussion about how to make this year different.

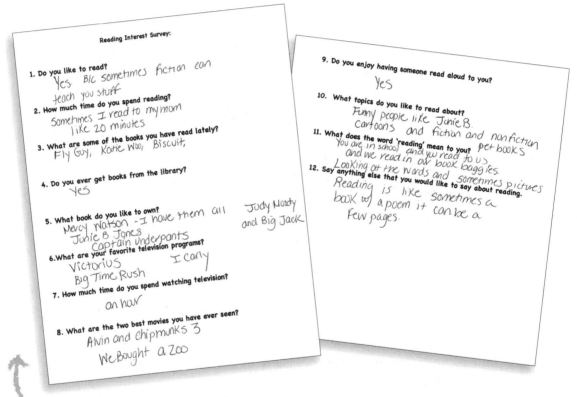

Reading Interest Survey:

1. Do you like to read?
   Yes. B/c sometimes fiction can teach you stuff

2. How much time do you spend reading?
   Sometimes I read to my mom like 20 minutes.

3. What are some of the books you have read lately?
   Fly Guy, Katie Woo, Biscuit,

4. Do you ever get books from the library?
   Yes

5. What book do you like to own?
   Mercy Watson - I have them all   Judy Moody
   Junie B Jones   and Big Jack
   Captain Underpants

6. What are your favorite television programs?
   Victorius   I carly
   Big Time Rush

7. How much time do you spend watching television?
   an hour

8. What are the two best movies you have ever seen?
   Alvin and chipmunks 3
   We Bought a Zoo

9. Do you enjoy having someone read aloud to you?
   Yes

10. What topics do you like to read about?
    Funny people like Junie B.
    Cartoons and fiction and nonfiction

11. What does the word 'reading' mean to you? Pet books
    You are in school and you read to us
    and we read in our book baggies.
    Looking at the words and sometimes pictures

12. Say anything else that you would like to say about reading.
    Reading is like sometimes a
    book w/ a poem it can be a
    few pages.

Figure 1.4 A reading interest inventory asks questions about a student's interests, habits, and attitudes around reading. There are many premade lists of questions that you can pull from by doing a quick Internet search, or you can make your own. You could also consider asking students to write you a letter about their interests and habits as readers, instead of answering a series of questions. For children in grades K and 1, I often ask the questions during a conference and record their answers, as you see in this figure. For students in grades 2 and up, I can give this inventory to the whole class at once and have them record their answers. Be careful that you ask questions in ways that are not leading, but are instead open-ended, such as "How do you feel about reading?" "Are there any books you like to read?" "Where do you like to read?" "Does anyone read to you outside of school?" and "Do you read to anyone?"

Even when squeezing every ounce of data from book logs and inventories as a teacher, I was left feeling still at an uncomfortable distance from knowing my students' engagement as readers. I developed another measure I call the **engagement inventory** as a kidwatching tool (see Figure 1.5) to quantitatively discover time on task and observable reading behaviors (Serravallo 2010).

Engagement Inventory

Names	12:35 (10 minutes)	12:45 (20 minutes)	12:55 (30 minutes)	1:00 (35 mintues)	notes
Abigail	R		S		
Alex		W		T	
August	T	W	Look in book bag		
Cameron	W	(looks tired)			
Carlo			T	C / S	
Chloe	R				
Eisley	T	T	C	T	
Ella F.					
Ella R.	R		R		
Emma					
Jonathan					
Julia	R	Switched books	S		
Julian					
Kenan					
Layla	R				
Lorent	W	W (head down)	T	C	
Monica				C	
Phoebe	T				
Ross		R			
Sammi	C		T		
Shaina		R			
Syanne		R			
Thayer	R		S		
Tyler D.		C		W	
Tyler L.	T	T	Switched books		
Zoe					

W = window   T = looking at teacher   R = reaching to text   S = smiling   C = chatting w/ neighbor

Figure 1.5 An engagement inventory is essentially a system to record student behaviors as they read. To complete this, you'll kidwatch—spend time literally just watching your students—recording what you see for an entire independent reading period, instead of conferring or pulling small groups. Record anything you notice that might be an important key to understanding what kids do as they are reading; for second graders, this might mean noticing avoidance behaviors such as going to the bathroom or getting up to get drinks of water every few minutes, distractibility, or how often they stop to jot a thought on a sticky note. For kindergarteners, it might mean noticing if a student finishes reading a book before beginning a new one, or looking at how long a student stays with a page before turning to a new one in an emergent storybook, or how long a child can read independently before sliding out of his chair to show a funny picture to his partner. Feel free to create your own coding system for recording behaviors that makes sense to you, and matches the types of behaviors of students at the age you teach.

To read more about engagement, see:

- Allington's (2011) *What Really Matters for Struggling Readers*

- Cunningham and Allington's (2010) *Classrooms That Work*

- Guthrie and Wigfield's (1997) *Reading Engagement*

- Routman's (1994) *Invitations*

ACTION ⟶ *Jot Down Your Ideas*

To borrow from renowned writing educator Carl Anderson (2000), I ask, "How's it going?" As you consider engagement and the three tools (**book logs, interest inventories**, and the **engagement inventories**) I've discussed, what resonates? What might you want to try first? Are their current students who come to mind you want to attend to first?

Write notes here:

_____

_____

_____

_____

Assessing Reading Fluency

Assessing a child's fluency is less straightforward than it would seem, because there is a chicken-and-egg relationship between fluency and comprehension. Beginning around level D/E, to read fluently a reader needs to understand what she's reading. But to understand the text, a reader needs to be able to read it fluently. At beginning reading levels, students aren't expected to read with some fluency on a first reading, but by level C they should work to be able to read with some fluency on a reread. Therefore, assessing fluency for most kindergarten teachers wouldn't happen until midyear for a majority of the class.

Reading rate or speed is one piece of the fluency puzzle. You can quickly gauge a child's rate by asking him to read for one minute, and record how many words he is able to read in that time, giving you a word per minute rate.

It's helpful to also consider accuracy, automaticity, expression (prosody), and parsing (phrasing) and take note of each aspect (Kuhn 2008).

A record of a child's oral reading can give helpful information about fluency. This can be obtained through by taking a **fluency record** (Figure 1.6) or a running record (Figure 1.8), in the context of any oral reading during a conference, shared reading lesson, or partnership reading.

Fluency Terms and Definitions

- *Accuracy* refers to the reader's ability to identify words correctly.

- *Automaticity* is the reader's ability to recognize words right away, without having to apply any strategies to figure them out. A reader can have a perfect accuracy rate, but not be very automatic. This would sound belabored and choppy.

- *Parsing* refers to a reader's ability to accurately break up, or phrase, longer sentences into syntactically appropriate phrase units. To do this accurately, a reader often needs to have some felt sense of how English syntax works, with phrases and clauses as parts of longer sentences. It may also mean that the reader is able to pay attention to medial punctuation like commas, semicolons, and dashes. If a reader reads without attention to correct phrases, comprehension could be altered. Consider Lynne Truss' (2006) clever picture books about grammar such as *Eats, Shoots & Leaves*. These books have the same phrase or sentence with and without a comma to teach children about the importance of these small marks on meaning.

- *Prosody* is a reader's ability to apply the appropriate amount of stress, emphasis, and intonation so that the reading sounds like how we talk. Without strong prosody, reading can sound monotonous and can even cause the reader to lose meaning.

Sugar Cakes Cyril by **Phillis Gershator**

(Mondo Publishing 1996)

Since Cyril/was the big brother/ he was/supposed to be the Big Helper/ But it seemed/like he was always/in the way/ If he poured the milk,/ it spilled/ If he shut the door, it slammed./

And now/ when he handed his mother/the baby powder/he dropped it,/ and the top fell off./The powder spilled out onto the floor/ It puffed up/into the air/and made them all cough/

"Go outside/ Cyril,/ his mother snapped/

"I thought/I was your Big Helper."/

"I don't need a helper right now,/ she said,/coughing/She finished / diapering the baby/and tried to clean up the powder/with a damp rag/

"Just go outside."/

Figure 1.6 Instead of listening only for miscues while a child reads aloud, listen with an ear toward fluency to take a fluency record. Make a slash mark each time you hear a student pause. Record information about the student's intonation or expression. This can be done as its own assessment or part of a running record (Figure 1.8). If done as part of a running record, you may ask a student to read aloud a portion of the text as you listen for miscues, and then another portion to listen for fluency. At lower levels where students' word per minute rate is slower, you will probably be able to record both simultaneously.

Because automaticity is an important part of being able to read fluently, it's important and helpful for children to have a bank of sight words. These are words that the student will know automatically, without having to figure them out. It's helpful for students to know words on sight that are **high-frequency words** (Figure 1.7). High-frequency words are those words that appear most frequently in text. For example, a beginning reader who knows *the, and, I, me, to, go, a, an* will be in a better position than one who knows *dog, cat, mom, dad, fish* simply because she will encounter these words more often in the books she's reading.

Name: Kristine			
	Date: 9/15	Date: 10/25	Date: 11/15
the	✓		
of	"if"	✓	
and	✓		
a	✓		
to	✓		
in	✓		
is	✓		
you	—	✓	
that	—	✓	
it	✓		
he	—	✓	
for	—	✓	
was	—	✓	
on	✓		
are	—	✓	
as	—	✓	
with	—	"want"	✓
his	—	"hit"	✓
they	—	—	✓
at	✓		
be	✓		

Figure 1.7 Create a list for the student and another for yourself on which to record the student's responses. Consider having separate pages for each word list, beginning with the most simple and most frequent words (this can be found by googling "Dolch" or "high-frequency words" or by visiting www.readingandwritingproject.com and looking under Assessments). Only consider the word known when the child can read it automatically, on sight. If a child starts to try to "sound out" or "chunk" the word to figure it out, record it as unknown and move on to the next word.

the	of	and
a	to	in
is	you	that
it	he	for
was	on	are
as	with	his
they	at	be

ACTION ⟶ *Jot Down Your Ideas*

As you consider fluency and the **fluency record** and **high-frequency word assessment**, what's on your mind? Do you feel this is an area that you'd want to look at with particular readers, right away? Do you already use assessments that allow you to look at your students' fluency? If so, are those helpful at looking at the same aspects of fluency as discussed in this chapter?

Write notes here:

_____

_____

_____

_____

To read more about fluency, see:

- Fountas and Pinnell's (2006) *Teaching for Comprehending and Fluency*

- Kuhn's (2008) *The Hows and Whys of Fluency Instruction*

- Rasinski's (2010) *The Fluent Reader*

Assessing Print Work/Decoding

When we look at a child's work through the lens of print work/decoding, we are training our attention to the work that students do when they come upon unfamiliar words in a text and what they do to figure out what those words say.

When children begin reading, many start by "reading" a story that they know well, turning the pages and telling the story from the pictures but sounding as if they were attending to print (Sulzby 1994). As you would suppose, this early reading behavior occurs primarily with familiar books that parents and teachers have read aloud to them.

After time in these emergent storybooks readers begin to be ready to use visual sources of information. Reading Recovery, Developmental Reading Assessment (DRA), and Irene Fountas and Gay Su Pinnell all have systems for leveling texts based on qualitative measures that help teachers introduce texts at a developmentally appropriate rate and within students' zones of proximal development.

At the most beginning levels, for example, Fountas and Pinnell (F&P) Text Level Gradient levels A and B, students begin understanding one-to-one matching and tracking the print with their finger and their eyes, left to right, following a pattern, and making sure their reading matches a picture. Beginning at level C, readers need to integrate the "graphophonic source of information," or information about letters and sounds, along with their knowledge of meaning and syntax.

When Is It Time to Begin Taking Running Records (And Move Children into Leveled Books)?

There are a number of indicators—both from reading and in writing—that will help you know when to begin administering and evaluating student's running records:

- It's possible for an adult (besides the child's teacher) to read back his writing.
- The writing shows a concept of word, with spacing.
- The child hears and is able to record beginning and ending sounds when writing.
- The child understands that print holds meaning, and can read back her writing.
- The child knows almost all of the letters and sounds the letters make (see, letter-sound ID assessment, page 4).
- The child knows about ten high-frequency sight words (see Figure 1.7).
- The child can read back a familiar text from shared reading.
- The child has moved into the last stage(s) of emergent reading (see emergent reading/writing chart in Appendix D).

Keep in mind that some children come into kindergarten already reading, many students will first be ready to read A- and B-level books for the first time around January or February of their kindergarten year, and still others won't be ready until June. It's more important to look for these indicators than think about a time in your yearly curriculum.

Placing children in leveled books too early can mean that they start to develop habits that are unhelpful in the long term. Ideally, you want a child to begin level A and B books and plan to stay in those levels for only a few weeks a piece, moving quickly to level C. This is because at level A and B students are working more on behaviors— moving left to right across the page, one-to-one matching, using the picture to figure out unknown words, and so on (see Appendix D for more detail on levels A and B) and integrating their meaning and syntactic sources of information. It isn't until level C that students need to begin integrating the visual source of information, using letters in the words. Staying too long (i.e., months and months) at levels A and B could teach children to ignore the print—the opposite of what we want in developing readers!

Beginning readers will check the picture to be sure they understand what's happening, and, still following a pattern, arrive at an unknown word. They'll use their knowledge of the alphabet and the sounds that letters make (letter-sound relationships) to begin to figure out what that word might be. As levels increase, so does the need to problem solve on the word level. Readers need to take on blends and digraphs, then later prefixes and suffixes, and multisyllabic words.

Print work is best assessed and taught in the context of meaning, so that a reader is constantly practicing his ability to integrate what he knows about letters and sounds (visual), with what is happening in the story (meaning), and how language works (syntax). A record of oral reading, such as a **running record** (see Figure 1.8), will give a teacher great information about a reader's print work strategies in the context of real reading.

Figure 1.8 You can take a running record on a blank piece of paper, on a typed copy of what the student is reading, or on a running record form as seen in this figure. As the student reads, you'll use a shorthand to record what you hear (see Figure 1.9). For words read correctly, you can make a check mark. When a child says something different from what is on the page, you'll want to record what the child says above what the text says on your record. This includes insertions, deletions, sounding out behavior, appeals for help, repetitions, and alternate pronunciations of the word.

It takes time to become facile with taking running records. See Marie Clay's book *Running Records for Classroom Teachers* (2000) for more practice with the process. See also Figure 1.9 for commonly used shorthand developed by Marie Clay (2000). See also the continuation of the running record—the comprehension component—within the next section, in Figure 1.13.

Running Record Sheet © 2005 by Marie M. Clay from *An Observation Survey of Early Literacy Achievement*, Third Edition (2013). Published by Global Education Systems Ltd. Reprinted by permission of the author's estate.

Analyzing an instructional-level running record is often much more revealing than an independent-level running record. Think about it, when the child reads with 98 percent accuracy, you might have only a couple of miscues to analyze. But when the child reads at 92 percent accuracy, there will be more miscues. When there are more miscues to analyze, patterns can be revealed that might otherwise be obscured. Therefore, when you're doing a running record, be sure to have the child read a text one level above that which he can read independently.

Running-Record Note-Taking	
✓	word read correctly
Mother (word read by student) Mom (word in text)	word read incorrectly
M-m-mahh-mom Mom	sounding out behavior
Mother SC Mom	self-correction
- mom	deletion (student skips a word)
mom -	insertion
Mother A Mom	appeal for help
Mother Mom T	teacher told student word
Mother R	student repeats

Figure 1.9 Shorthand Commonly Used for Running Records The table shows a coding system to use when taking running records that is recommended by Marie Clay (2000). Use this, or make your own, but try to be as consistent within your school as possible. When the coding of running records is consistent, all support teachers and classroom teachers from room to room will be able to use a common language to interpret a child's miscues and self-corrections.

ACTION ➤ *Jot Down Your Ideas*

As you consider print work/decoding and the **running record** I've discussed, what resonates? Do you feel this is an area you've focused much on? What new ideas do you have about how decoding may or may not be an important part of reading instruction in your class?

Write notes here:

_____

_____

_____

_____

To read more about assessing and teaching print work strategies, see:

- Clay's (1991) *Becoming Literate*

- Clay's (2000) *Running Records for Classroom Teachers*

- Fountas and Pinnell's (2009) *When Readers Struggle*

- McGill-Franzen's (2006) *Kindergarten Literacy*

Assessing Reading Comprehension

Without comprehension, reading is just saying words. To truly read is to uncover meaning within a text, understand what the author is saying, and have your own reactions and responses to it.

Before children can even read conventionally, we can start teaching them the importance of comprehension. When she was two, I probably read upward of five books a day to my daughter. We'd snuggle into a rocking chair, give the book our attention, and listen to the author's words. We'd stop at places to talk about what was happening, we'd laugh when a character did silly stuff, and she occasionally reacted with an "I never knew that! Did you know that, Mama?" when we read something interesting. She knew maybe three letters of the alphabet (on a good day) at that time, but she understood that when you read a book, you strive to understand it.

Somehow, sometimes, something goes awry with students and they misunderstand what it means to read. Some children have gotten a message that saying the words right, reading at a certain speed, or making your reading sound good is all that matters. This is why work done in the primary years can build a strong foundation of understanding that reading is always tied to meaning making. Consequently, comprehension falters. Or, other times there is something standing in the way of a child understanding a text, such as limited prior knowledge about the topic or a memory issue that makes it challenging to carry information from one page to the next.

In an educational context, *comprehension* is often used as an umbrella term and includes a handful of skills and strategies that readers use in concert. Authors like Keene and Zimmermann (2007), Miller (2013), Pearson and colleagues (1992), and Harvey and Goudvis (2007) have written about these aspects of comprehension and encourage teachers to make this the reading curriculum in grades K–8 (Pearson et al. 1992). The goal is not to assess for and teach children to be overly metacognitive when naming their process, but instead to be aware of these areas of comprehension so that we can find ways to better support readers' deepening understandings of texts. These areas are:

- activating prior knowledge before, during, and after reading a text
- determining the most important themes and ideas in a text
- creating visual and sensory images before, during, and after reading a text
- asking questions
- drawing inferences
- retelling and synthesizing
- using fix-up strategies when comprehension breaks down

Keene and Zimmermann and others refer to these as "strategies," though in my community at the Teachers College Reading and Writing Project, we call them "skills" (Afflerbach, Pearson, and Paris 2008; Serravallo 2010). Regardless of what they are called, what's important is that we have an eye on how well children understand a text. We can use these subcategories of comprehension to see the areas where children are strongest, and those they need the most support in shoring up.

Determining what meaning children are making in a text is one of the trickiest parts of assessing reading. But in fact, it's the thrust of what's called for in the Reading Informational Texts and Reading Literature sections of the Common Core State Standards (2010). Comprehension can, at times, be invisible. In our attempts to make reading comprehension visible—by having students write about, speak about, or answer questions about their reading—we are limited by the student's ability to represent her understanding using one of those formats. In other words, when students struggle to use the format, the depth of their comprehension may be obscured.

For example, when we ask a child to retell a story aloud, and she has difficulty doing so, it could be that she didn't understand the story enough to retell it, or it could be that she has trouble verbally expressing herself. When we ask a student to stop and jot ideas about a character in a text, and it appears as though his answers are very basic, is that an indication that he is thinking in a very simplistic way about his characters or that he has trouble expressing himself in writing?

The best we can do when assessing comprehension is to try to sample student understanding in a variety of ways. We may ask a student questions during a conference and record her answers in writing in our conferring notes. We may ask a student who is able to **stop and jot** as he reads a short text or whole book independently (see Figures 1.10 and 1.11). We could listen in as a child discusses a book with a peer and transcribe the **conversation** (see Figure 1.14). This data collection method is useful for assessing readers at all levels, even those who are working with emergent storybooks at the beginning of kindergarten. Looking back at this transcript will give you information about the kinds of comprehension strategies students are using and how well they are using them.

A **running record** can also offer us insight into comprehension, if the practice of taking a running record involves asking the student to retell and answer some direct comprehension questions afterward (see Figure 1.12). We could read aloud to the child and ask him to **stop and jot** (appropriate for most students by late first grade) or **turn and talk** (for those students whose responses you'd want to transcribe) during the reading (see Figure 1.13).

Figure 1.10 Good for readers at levels K and up, try taking a short story or typed-up picture book and insert questions and prompts. As the student reads, he stops and jots responses and reactions to the questions and prompts. This assessment was developed by the Teachers College Reading and Writing Project and can be downloaded from their website under Assessments at www.readingandwritingproject.com. Many teachers find these tools to be helpful formative or summative assessments of a student's work within a unit of study.

Level K Story

A Tough Day for Thomas
By Shannon Rigney Keane

Thomas often lost things. Sometimes, he lost his toys. Sometimes, he lost books. Sometimes, he lost things that you might think would be difficult to lose. One night at dinner, he tried to take a bite of mashed potatoes but he had lost his fork!

1A. Close Reading/Monitoring for sense:
What have you learned about Thomas so far?

He loses things a lot

Losing things did not bother Thomas. His parents shook their heads at him. "Good thing your shoes are tied on to your feet," they told him, "or you would never make it to school!" But he just laughed and said, "I'm sure I'll find it sooner or later."

And he would play with a different toy, or read a different book – or eat with his fingers! – until he found the thing he had lost. Often, he found the lost thing in a very unusual place. A plastic dinosaur in the freezer, his favorite book under the bathroom sink, his fork in the dog's bowl.

1 B. Close Reading/Monitoring for sense:
What more have you learned about Thomas?

most of the time he finds what he has lost

continues

Figure 1.10 *continued*

One morning, Thomas woke up and turned over in his bed so he could look out the window. To his surprise, he saw a big yellow truck in front of the house next door, his best friend Robby's house. There were men carrying boxes... Thomas jumped out of bed and ran to the kitchen in his pajamas.

His parents were sitting at the table drinking hot coffee out of mugs. He asked them what was going on, and why there was a truck outside of his best friend Robby's house.

2. Prediction:
What do you think will happen in the rest of the story? What makes you think this?

robby is moving. because men carring boxes

His parents looked at each other, then they looked at him. His mother said, "Robby's family has to move to a different town. He came over this morning to say goodbye. I told him you would come over as soon as you got up. Go put your clothes on so you can see Robby before he goes."

Thomas had a funny feeling in his stomach as he put on his clothes. The funny feeling got worse when he saw Robby's empty house, and gave Robby a hug, and watched Robby's dad drive the family away in their red car. Thomas watched them drive away behind the yellow moving truck until they turned a corner and he could not see them anymore. Then he went back to his own house, with the funny feeling in his stomach.

For a long time, Thomas sat on the steps in front of his house. He could hear his family moving around inside his house. He saw other kids playing. He knew some of them, and they waved at him. He waved back. He thought of Robby. His mom sat next to him on the steps. For a few minutes, they did not say anything.

3. Envisionment:
Picture what is happening right now. Describe it using as many details as you can.

he is sad that robby moved and that means he can not play every day.

Then, his mom said, "I know it's sad when someone we like goes away, but you have other friends."

Thomas said, "But I don't have any other Robby's. Robby has been my best friend for a long time."

"Yes," his mom said, "things that are important, like friends, take time. It will take time to make a new best friend. But you will."

Thomas thought about other things he had lost, and how he always found them sooner or later in unusual places, like the freezer, or under the bathroom sink, or in the dog's bowl. Losing a friend was different. He did not have another friend to play with that would be just the same.

4. Interpretation
What can you learn from Thomas' experience?

if you lose something you can always get it back\find a nother way.

Figure 1.11 For readers at levels J/K and above, an assessment of whole-book comprehension can help us to collect information about students' understanding across an entire book. For narrative, a student would read an entire chapter book and answer questions about plot and setting, character, vocabulary and figurative language, and themes and ideas. For informational texts, while reading an entire book, a student would answer questions about the main idea, key details, vocabulary, and text features as he reads. This assessment can capture how well students can accumulate information and how well they are able to handle the text complexities of a given level (Serravallo 2012, 2013).

Form 1 (top left)

Student Response Form

Student's name ___Allan___   Grade ___First___

Your teacher wants to learn more about you as a reader. Here are some directions to remember:

+ Please complete this assessment on your own. Do not ask for help or use anything (dictionaries, websites, etc.) to help you.
+ Each time you read, please fill in your reading log below.
+ When you reach a page with a sticky note, read to the bottom of the page.
+ Stop and answer the question on your response form. Include as much detail as you can from the book to support your answer. (It is fine to reread, but do not read ahead.)
+ Put the sticky note back in the book.
+ Keep reading!

| READING LOG | | | | | Teacher: Please fill out. | |
Date	Start Time	End Time	Start Page	End Page	Total Time	Total Pages
5/25	9:45	10:15	1	56	30	56
			Total		30	56

Independent Reading Assessment: Fiction © 2012 by Jennifer Serravallo • Scholastic Inc.   **1**

Form 2 (top right)

1. PAGE 7 What kind of person is Dolores?

Bully

2. PAGE 10 What kind of person is Andy Shane?   E P A I

He doesn't like school and he dosen't like Dolores.

3. PAGE 14 What are some problems that Andy is having?   E P A I

Dolores is calling out.

4. PAGE 24 What is the "Granny Webb Stare"?   E P A I

She sneesd a big bogger

E P A I

Independent Reading Assessment: Fiction © 2012 by Jennifer Serravallo • Scholastic Inc.   **2**

Form 3 (bottom left)

5. PAGE 33 How is Andy's problem getting worse?

Dolores is getting meaner.

E P A I

6. PAGE 40 Why does Granny start singing and dancing?

to showa verb

E P A I

7. PAGE 45 In this part, what does Dolores's "face turned the color of a fire ant" mean?

Dolores's face turned red.

E P A I

8. PAGE 51 How is Andy acting differently than he did before?

Andy is feeling happy

E P A I

Independent Reading Assessment: Fiction © 2012 by Jennifer Serravallo • Scholastic Inc.   **3**

Form 4 (bottom right)

9. PAGE 56 What is a lesson Andy learns by the end of the story?

Andy learned to talk to dolorest

E P A I

Reflection

Was this book easy, just right, or too hard? __just right__

How do you know? __it's just right because it seems like my reading level.__

Did you like this book? __yes__

Why or why not? __Why because it was very funny__

Would you choose another book like this from the library? __NO__

Why or why not? __Why not because this might be my favorite book now.__

Independent Reading Assessment: Fiction © 2012 by Jennifer Serravallo • Scholastic Inc.   **4**

Figure 1.12 After taking an oral running record at any level, standard practice is to ask the child to retell what she's read, and then ask a small handful of follow-up comprehension questions, some literal and some inferential. Most commercially produced running records, such as the DRA (Beaver 2006) or F&P's *Benchmark Assessment System 1* (2010) include these questions. If you'll be taking a running record as a student reads a book from your classroom library, you'll need to create your own.

Dylan — 4/12

Retell: Nick was going to go to bed. He was missing something. He wanted to read a story.

Q's —
1. What was the book about? Magic fish.
2. How did Nick feel about it? Liked it.
3. What else does Nick's mom do? Turns on light (looking back) goodnight kiss
4. Why does he ask her to do all of those things? Doesn't want to go to bed.

Jake is a trouble maker. I think this because he is the class clown.

Why is Miss Bruce so mean

Is Jake a fast reader now?

Will Mrs. Brattle now be mean?

Figure 1.13 By the end of first grade, most students can quickly jot at least a word or phrase. During a read-aloud, you may preplan a few places as stop-and-jot spots. After planning questions that assess particular reading skills, you can ask students to stop and record an answer on a sticky note or piece of paper. For example, if you're trying to assess the students' abilities to visualize you might say, "Describe what you're picturing here." To assess inference, you might say, "What kind of person is the character?" It's also helpful to look at the quick jots students write on sticky notes in their own books as they read independently. In kindergarten or early first grade, before students can quickly jot their thinking on paper, you may still consider planning and asking questions during read-alouds, but instead of jotting, ask students to turn and talk. As they talk, you and any other adults who may be in the room with you can record some of what you hear students saying. This figure shows four separate jots by the same reader at the end of his first-grade year.

ACTION ➤ *Jot Down Your Ideas*

As you consider comprehension and making student thinking visible through **whole-book assessments, short-passage assessments**, and **conversation**, what do you think you'll try first? What systems and structures are already in place in your classroom to help make your students' comprehension visible?

Write notes here:

_____

_____

_____

_____

To read more about comprehension, see:

- Collins' (2004) *Growing Readers*

- Fountas and Pinnell's (2010) *The Continuum of Literacy Learning*

- Harvey and Goudvis' (2007) *Strategies That Work*

- Keene and Zimmermann's (2007) *Mosaic of Thought*

- Keene et al's (2011) *Comprehension Going Forward*

- Miller's (2013) *Reading with Meaning*

- Parsons' (2010) *First Grade Readers*

- Taberski's (2010) *Comprehension from the Ground Up*

- Zimmermann and Hutchins' (2003) *7 Keys to Comprehension*

Assessing Conversation

Student conversations about their reading—whether with a reading partner, a book club, or during a whole-class conversation—give teachers a window into students' understanding. As I've mentioned in the previous section on comprehension, we can transcribe these conversations and reflect on them through the lens of comprehension: what does the transcript reveal that a student understands or doesn't understand?

Conversation itself is also a skill. As the Speaking and Listening strand of the Common Core State Standards (2010) articulate, there are many aspects to engaging in thoughtful conversation (www.corestandards.org). Some highlights from the first-grade standards, for example, are:

- Follow agreed upon rules of discussion.
- Listen to others with care.

- Speak one at a time about the topic(s) under discussion.
- Respond to the comments of others through multiple exchanges.
- Ask questions to clear up confusion.

It is essential, then, that we provide opportunities across the day for our students to engage in meaningful conversation: about topics of importance to the classroom community, about books read together as a class and independently with partners and clubs, about their writing, about math, and so on. As students speak and listen, it's just as important for us as teachers to listen and assess. I am in the habit of taking notes during **whole-class conversations** (see Figure 1.14), **one-on-one**, and **small-group conversations**. I use these notes as assessments from which to craft goals, and develop teaching and learning opportunities for students.

Figure 1.14 As students speak about a read-aloud as a whole class, I try to hang back and take notes about what students are doing. I record who speaks and who stays silent (see the checks around a circle on the left). The circle represents the seating position of each student. Every time a child speaks during the conversation, I will make a check mark next to his or her initials/name on his/her spot on the circle, and write a brief transcription of what was said. I record how I intervene to provide instructional support (see the transcript on the right). I can then return to this transcript and read through the lens of noticing what they are doing as conversationalists, with the aim of setting goals for my class' work during talk time.

Baseball Ballerina   9/25

A.M. – shouldn't have to listen to her mom.
A.F. – agree. Mom should let her play baseball.
I – yeah but she's a girl, so...
M.L. – Mom wants her to do what other girls do.
S.A. – It doesn't matter.
R – Like in Oliver Button. He wanted to dance.
G. – yeah. Not like other boys.
R. – so BB's mom should talk to O.B.'s dad!
P.V. – yeah! Good idea.
P.P. – what does your mom make you do that you don't like?
M.P. – my mom doesn't care abt. "boy vs. girl stuff"
R. – mine too.
M.P. – I play soccer, so what?
G. – soccer's not girl stuff or boy stuff. It's for both.
M.P. – I think so, too. I agree with Gregory.

ACTION → Jot Down Your Ideas

As you consider conversation, reflect for a moment about the time your students have to talk in class, and whether you tend to use those talk opportunities also as assessment opportunities. What will you try from this section?

Write notes here:

_____

_____

_____

_____

To read more about conversation, see:

- Bomer and Bomer's (2001) *For a Better World*

- Collins' (2008) *Reading for Real*

- Johnston's (2004) *Choice Words*

- Nichols' (2006) *Comprehension Through Conversation*

Assessing Writing Engagement

Just as we considered reading engagement as an important factor before launching into the quality of a students' reading work, so too should we consider writing engagement. A child's attitudes toward, beliefs about, and desire to write are the stepping-stones to producing good writing.

We can also look at students' habits and process and consider:

- volume of writing (how much a student produces in a given time)
- motivation to write
- whether a student understands, and uses, a writing process

To read more about ways to support writing engagement, look to:

- Mermelstein's (2013) *Self-Directed Writers*

- Calkins' and colleagues (2013) *Units of Study in Opinion, Information, and Narrative Writing*

I recommend kidwatching and completing an **engagement inventory** (see Figure 1.5) for writing workshop just like you would in reading workshop. Having students keep a writer's notebook and **examining writing volume** over time is a way to study whether volume of writing is stagnant or improving. Also, encouraging students to hold on to all the parts of their process—entries in the notebook, drafts, evidence of revision on the draft or with add-on pieces such as sticky notes—as well as a published piece will give a bigger picture of what they understand about the writing process and will also send the message that process as well as product is valued in your classroom.

Assessing Qualities of Good Writing

When I was a new classroom teacher I spent three hours once a week studying student writing with Carl Anderson while he was in the midst of writing the book *Assessing Writers* (Anderson 2005). Carl would put up a piece of writing and we'd have to say at least ten things the student was doing well. This was harder to do for some pieces than for others! Then, we'd shift our thinking and try to name out every possibility for growth for that student. Then we'd do it again. And again. This experience of repeated practice, under the tutelage of a master teacher, equipped me with a framework I use every time I approach a piece of student writing.

Whether I'm looking at a piece of **narrative** (personal narrative, memoir, fiction), **informational** (all-about book, content essay), or **opinion** (persuasive essay, review, speech) writing, I apply what are commonly known as the qualities of good writing:

- meaning
- structure/organization
- elaboration/detail
- conventions

In a way, assessing writing can feel a bit more accessible than assessing reading because we have a visual artifact that we can pack in our bags and take home and something right on the child's desktop to look at when we confer. Still, consciously choosing lenses for assessing writing is essential to be able to determine importance and to know what to teach first. Also, we need to provide varied opportunities for students to write and look at those different types of writing alongside one another.

Some writing we are assessing may have been through an entire writing cycle (see Figure 1.15). If working within a writing workshop, students receive a daily minilesson as well as one-on-one and small-group support with their writing. The final product should be fairly polished as it represents work over a good amount of time, and guided practice from a teacher.

Independent Writing in Early Kindergarten

Even before students are able to hear the sounds in words and match those sounds to letters, recording what they want to write, they can still "write." Teaching students to say a story aloud and then record their story on paper using representational drawings is important to helping them internalize story sense and feel ownership over their work. Teaching students to write their stories from the first days of school in kindergarten can help you, as the teacher, identify many of the qualities of good writing (meaning, structure, and elaboration) that are not word-dependent.

You may begin the year with giving students a blank piece of paper, maybe one with a line on the bottom of the page. Students can think of a story and then "write" the story by drawing a picture. Some will use the line to record letter strings, and others will attempt some words. Still others will ask for a couple more pieces of paper and will attempt to write a multi-page piece. Within a couple of months, many teachers find it helpful to offer all children multi-page booklets, to teach children about the structure of a story. At first, it may be two pages representing beginning and end. Later, you may introduce three pages—beginning, middle, and end. As students' knowledge of letter and sound develops, you can also begin encouraging them to label their pictures, at times with the support of a personal alphabet chart. For more information about early writing, see Ray's *In Pictures and In Words* (2010) and Ray and Glover's *Already Ready* (2008).

On-demand writing is writing that is completed in one to three sittings and asks students to go through the entire process of planning, drafting, revising, and editing independently (see Figure 1.16). Without minilessons or conferring, this shows us the writing that students can do independently. It also is an interesting assessment of what students understand about process. You may want to offer an open-ended prompt to get kids started:

- **Narrative:** Think of something important that happened to you. Tell the story of what happened with as much detail as you can.
- **Opinion:** Think of something you have strong feelings about. Write a piece convincing someone about what you think.
- **Informational:** Think of something you feel you know a lot about. Write a piece teaching me what you know about it.

Figure 1.15 These sample pages represent the process of one student from Kristine Mraz's kindergarten classroom. The child first drew pictures to hold on to the important information she intended to write on each page. Then, she went back to write sentences on the lines below. Her class was working on elaboration, trying to write at least three facts per page. She went back and added extra sentences, sometimes even by adding flaps and strips (see the final couple of pages) when what she wanted to write exceeded the number of lines on the page. She does some minimal crossing out. This process, in addition to the qualities of good writing demonstrated in the final version, will be important to examine, as a child's writing process is sometimes tied to the quality of the work.

The amount of time a student takes to go through the entire process will vary by grade level and by the volume included within the piece. For example, a kindergartener in September may draw a picture to represent a story, and may or may not use a line at the bottom of a page to record a string of letters, a couple of words, or an attempt at a sentence. A second grader, on the other hand, may write a story across five pages in a booklet, with a small space for pictures and ten lines on the bottom of each page. A kindergartener would likely be able to produce the on-demand writing in one sitting; the second grader may take two or three workshop periods to take one piece through the writing process.

For both through-the-process and on-demand writing, you'll want to have an eye on your curriculum and make sure you're teaching a balance of informational, narrative, and opinion writing. The writing

samples you collect for the purpose of trying this protocol will depend on where you are in your current curriculum. It's important that the student work is current, and therefore it's unlikely that the student will have current work from all three domains of writing.

As you'll see in Chapter 3, and notice in Appendix D, student writing can help us to develop an understanding of not only the student as a writer, but also the student as a reader. Examining reading–writing connections gives us a more complete picture of a student. Crafting goals that are applicable to both reading and writing will help the student to have more depth to her work across the day and may ensure faster success with accomplishing a goal.

For a deeper, more controlled study of a student's grasp of one aspect of conventions, a student's spelling, you may choose to conduct a **spelling inventory** (Figure 1.17). Unlike a spelling test that asks children to memorize and then spell a collection of words usually with a common theme or common spelling feature, a spelling inventory is a diagnostic tool. A spelling inventory, such as Bear et al's (2011), offers students a variety of increasingly complex words to spell. Each word is aligned to a developmental spelling stage. The purpose of the inventory is to analyze which spelling *stage* the student is currently in so that the teacher may provide appropriate instruction within that stage. The purpose is not to simply test the student's ability to spell the set of words.

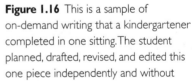

Figure 1.16 This is a sample of on-demand writing that a kindergartener completed in one sitting. The student planned, drafted, revised, and edited this one piece independently and without any support in the form of a minilesson, small-group instruction, or conferring.

When prompted "Tell me about your story" the child replied, "My friends are Jacob and Isabelle. See? I wrote "friends" [points under FDNS] and "I" for Isabelle and "J" for Jacob [points under letters]." When asked "What's happening in your picture?" the child replied, "He's smiling at me because I helped him out."

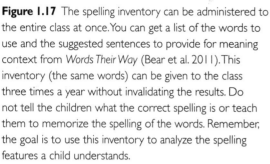

Figure 1.17 The spelling inventory can be administered to the entire class at once. You can get a list of the words to use and the suggested sentences to provide for meaning context from *Words Their Way* (Bear et al. 2011). This inventory (the same words) can be given to the class three times a year without invalidating the results. Do not tell the children what the correct spelling is or teach them to memorize the spelling of the words. Remember, the goal is to use this inventory to analyze the spelling features a child understands.

For example, in this assessment, the child's spelling of the word *fan* as *f-a-n-s* shows that the child understands initial consonant, final consonant, and the short vowel *a*. However, *pet* (#2) is spelled *p-a-t* and *dig* (#3) is spelled *d-a-g*, showing that the child needs continued practice with short vowels. He spells *hope* (#5) as *h-o-s-t* and *gum* as *g-o-a-t*, revealing he can also use more support with final consonants. Because final consonants precede short vowels in the developmental spelling progression, the teacher would place this student in a group with other children who will work with words to learn that feature. For more information, or for this specific list, see Bear et al (2011).

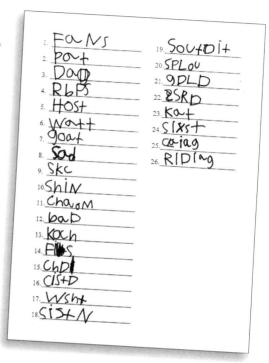

ACTION ⟶ *Jot Down Your Ideas*

As you consider qualities of good writing, what recent piece or pieces will you examine? Do you have any artifacts that could show process and/or engagement? How can you collect work that shows both **product** as well as **process**?

Write notes here:

_____

_____

_____

_____

To read more about the qualities of good writing, see:

- Anderson's (2005) *Assessing Writers*

- Bear et al.'s (2011) *Words Their Way*

- Calkins' and colleagues (2013) *Units of Study in Opinion, Information, and Narrative Writing*

- Fountas and Pinnell's (1998) *Word Matters*

⬚ Wrap-Up

As you read through this chapter, reflect on the types of student work you tend to have at-the-ready. This may give you some insight into your own instructional priorities. Alternatively, it may reflect the types of work you felt your students needed the most practice with based on prior assessments.

Either way, I encourage you to set aside some planning and teaching time to make sure you've got a good sense of your students as both readers and writers. Make sure you understand your students in terms of their process and their products. Make sure you're looking to see not only what they do, but how engaged they are while they do it.

⬚ What's Next?

In Chapter 2, we'll be taking the student work you've collected and studying it piece by piece to look for teaching opportunities. Make sure you've got a student's work to look at, and/or print out the work of another student, Emre, which is available at www.heinemann.com/products/E05300.aspx (click on the Companion Resources tab).

ACTION ⟶

- If you jotted down notes in each assessment lens section, skim them now and circle what strikes you as the most urgent action to take in your class or question to pursue. Perhaps think about a colleague you could team up with to collaborate on improving practices around assessing reading and/or writing.

- Collect artifacts to represent each assessment lens (ideally from the last couple of weeks) for at least one student. Keep in mind that some assessments relate to several lenses (for example, a running record can give you information about fluency, print work, and comprehension).

Chapter 2

Analyzing Data

MAKING DISCOVERIES FROM STUDENT WORK

One of my favorite parts of spending time with young children is the wonder, curiosity, and open-mindedness they bring to everything. We adults often will just glance at something quickly, register it in our minds as something we've seen before, and move along our merry way. But not children.

> It is a fine thing to have ability, but the ability to discover things in others is the true test.
> **—Lou Holtz**

I first noticed this about children from a teacher's perspective. Kids would rush through the classroom door after recess, breathless, excited to show me the rock/bug/stick/leaf they found outside, sharing observations and asking questions. But I don't think it really struck me in quite the same way until I experienced it from a parent's perspective. When my daughter was just two years old I can remember her asking me about the stars in a way that made me realize, *she's noticing them for the first time.* With that newness came close study, and thoughtfulness, and questions.

It's with that same spirit of marveling at the new that we can approach student work to learn about our students deeply and make discoveries about them. I'll teach you in this chapter how to work through step 2 of the protocol, analyzing data. We'll take each piece of student work and instead of just glancing quickly and drawing a single, quick conclusion, we'll lean in and look with the same spirit of curiosity and interest that our youngest students have taught us to have.

- Step 1: Collect data.
X •**Step 2: Analyze data.**
  - Step 3: Interpret data and establish a goal.
  - Step 4: Create an action plan.

Are you sitting with a stack of student work at your side? I hope so! Reading this chapter will be a lot more useful if you have these samples at the ready. Decide if you'll practice using Emre's work (see Appendix A at the back of this book, or www.heinemann.com /products/E05300.aspx) or your own student's work.

Here are some essential reminders about the work described in Chapter 1:

- Collect samples of students' reading and writing work.
- Use current work, from the last few weeks, that represents about the same period in time. This is important because a student can show different strengths and needs if one were to look at artifacts that were collected many weeks apart.
- Be sure that you have samples that allow you to evaluate through each of the five lenses for reading (engagement, comprehension, print work, fluency, conversation) and writing work that shows process as well as product; one student work example to represent each lens is sufficient, and some work will help you understand students through more than one lens.

In the sections that follow, I provide practical help with looking closely at each artifact to discover a student's strengths and potential areas for growth. I offer key questions to ask of the work, and some of the "look-fors," so that you can extrapolate the ideas that I have about the work of one student—a first grader named Marelle. I summarize my thoughts about each piece of work in a table.

I gathered Marelle's work in May of her first-grade year. At that time she had made a great deal of progress in her language skills (she speaks Spanish as her first language) and literacy skills, yet was reading and writing below grade-level expectations. The look-fors and expectations I describe are to help you understand my thinking behind the work she's doing. Some readers of this book will be able to directly apply what I describe about Marelle to their own student.

However, because there is such variation across grades and across levels of reading and writing proficiency, I've also created tables for level bands A–B, C–D, and E–F (see Appendix D) to present descriptions of general behaviors and goals that we tend to look for within those levels, and the ways in which expectations for reading and writing might connect. In the same appendix I've also included a table of emergent reading behaviors to help frame your analysis of early kindergarten literacy. Of course, children's reading and writing growth doesn't develop in lockstep, and these tables are meant to be used as general guidelines, not checklists. They are also not everything you need to know at these levels, but instead are intended as a start to get you thinking. Please keep in mind that you should always plan to consult the resources and standards I mention throughout this chapter to make sure that your expectations are appropriate for the grade and developmental stage of the student you're studying.

My hope is that you'll try the process of analyzing student work samples alongside me as you read this chapter. I've included work from another student in Marelle's class, from the same time of year. His name is Emre and as you look at his work you'll see that his reading level and volume of writing indicate he seems to be exceeding grade-level expectations and his work tells a very different story than that of Marelle's. If you'd like to try this process with Emre's work, you'll want to have a copy ready. You can download his work samples from www.heinemann.com/products/E05300.aspx or find them in Appendix A. You can also find my commentary on Emre's work in the back of the book in Appendix A—but no peeking until you give it a try!

After walking through my analysis of Marelle and trying the work on your own with Emre, you may try this process with your own students' work. Where my evaluation of Marelle and Emre's work might seem drastically different than what you'd expect from either more emergent readers or more sophisticated readers, I've popped in notes or sidebars that may help you consider your own students' work in a more informed way. I encourage you to always consult grade-level expectations such as standards, and/or grade-specific materials such as Fountas and Pinnell's *The Continuum of Literacy Learning* (2010) and/or Calkins and colleagues' *Units of Study in Opinion, Information, and Narrative Writing* (2013).

After supporting hundreds of teachers with this process, I have found that one of the biggest advantages a teacher has is a deep knowledge of content. Although I do provide some support with the content you'll need, you may also use this chapter as a way to identify some gaps in your own content knowledge. When gaps occur, I encourage you to set a goal for your own learning and consult the resources I recommend in this chapter and in Chapter 1.

In this second step of the protocol, try to follow the advice of Peter Johnston (2004) and "notice and name" elements of your students' work. You may:

- Speak aloud, listing what you see. Be as precise as possible.
- Consider if what you see is evidence of a strength or a need.
- List observations in a chart, naming out strengths and potential areas for growth.

One important exercise is to make sure that the potential areas of growth we identify *are linked to the students' strengths*. That means we aren't looking for deficits in the absence of a noticeable strength. Instead, the teaching potential comes from noticing something that the student can already do. This will ensure that our ideas for teaching goals are those that are within the student's zone of proximal development (Vygotsky 1978).

Keep in mind that what a student exhibits as a strength in November may be very different from her strengths in May. A student's strengths and needs change and develop across the year, and, consequently, the process of evaluating data and goal setting based on that work is ongoing (see Figure 4.10 in Chapter 4).

If possible, work with colleagues as you analyze your students' work, because sometimes, knowing a student well can color what we see in the data. Trusted colleagues can bring invaluable insight and objectivity. Perhaps this could be work you do with a staff developer or literacy coach, or during a professional learning community meeting.

I recommend that you organize your conclusions and ideas into a simple table, such as the Table for Summarizing Analysis of Data (Figure 2.1) so that you may easily look across patterns and trends, which is coming in Chapter 3, step 3.

Table for Summarizing Analysis of Data

Tool	Strengths	Possibilities for Growth
Reading Log		
Writing about Reading		
Running Record		
Independent Reading Assessment		

Figure 2.1

One final quick word before we dive in—you're going to notice that you'll spend a long time on this part of the protocol. Don't panic! Although it's true that the work of analyzing each piece of data individually is not quick, the process you're going to experience here will pay off in a number of ways—both for your students' learning as well as for your own. Also, keep in mind that I have collected many more student work examples from this sample student than you'll need for your own student(s). In addition, consider that this process is one that you'll want to use at first with those students who puzzle you most. Finally, know that like anything, with practice, the process of analysis will become like second nature and you'll be able to move through it more quickly and easily.

ACTION →

Decide if you'll work through this chapter with Emre's work (available at www.heinemann.com /products/E05300.aspx) or with the work you've collected from a student you teach. Have it at your side. Also, photocopy the Table for Summarizing Analysis of Data available in Appendix C, or quickly make your own table similar to Figure 2.1 in a word-processing document.

Using the Engagement Inventory

The engagement inventory will give you helpful information about your students' behaviors during independent reading, even when independent reading time is spent doing emergent reading work in familiar storybooks. You can discover how well the student is able to settle into reading once the minilesson has ended, learn how long the student is able to sustain reading before losing attention, and begin to recognize the signs of engagement or distraction the student exhibits.

By using an engagement inventory, you can more accurately diagnose *if* a student has trouble with engagement, and *if so,* what sort of challenge the student faces.

What to Look For

In the left-hand column, you'll find questions you can ask yourself when looking at the engagement inventory. In the middle column, you'll find advice on a precise place to look on the work sample that will help answer those questions. In the right-hand column, you'll find an ideal student behavior. Compare this ideal to what you're seeing in the engagement inventory, and use it to help you fill out the strengths/areas for growth chart:

Engagement Inventory Look-Fors

Question to Ask	Where to Look	The Ideal
Can the student settle into reading right away, or does she take some time to get settled?	Look to see if you have marked in the first box that the student is doing something other than reading.	The student can get settled immediately. Keep in mind, though, that "settled" may involve some degree of wiggling when it comes to younger children.
Is the student is especially prone to distractions (i.e., noises outside the classroom, announcements, other students nearby) that interrupt reading for extended periods of time?	Look at places where you noted disengagement. Did anything happen at that time that might have caused it?	The student stays focused despite outside distractions. Or, the student is able to resettle after a brief distraction.
What signs of engagement might she exhibit?	Check the inventory for: laughing out loud, jotting an occasional symbol or word on a sticky note, making facial expressions, and so on.	The student shows some signs of engaged, interested reading as indicated by some observable emotional response.
How long can the student maintain focused, engaged reading?	Count the number of minutes in a stretch of engaged reading.	Students often alternate between independent reading and reading with a partner. Their total reading time should be around 35–40 minutes.*
What signs of disengagement does she exhibit?	Check the engagement inventory for writing on sticky notes more than reading, switching her book for a new one midchapter or midpage, staring out the window or watching the teacher, and so on.	The student does not show signs of disengagement. Or, when the student is disengaged, it is temporary and the student is able to quickly refocus.
Does she have strategies for reengaging with her reading once she becomes distracted?	Look to see how long the period of distraction lasts, and if there are any notes about what the student does after (i.e., flipping back a page to reread, doing a stretch, or breathing to refocus).	Distractions are few, and, when they occur, the student is able to quickly reengage with her reading.

*In second grade, children can typically work up to reading for a thirty- to thirty-five-minute stretch, and then partner time can be saved for the end of the workshop. The recommendation to alternate "private" or independent reading with partner reading is helpful for kindergarteners and first graders.

A Sample Analysis: Marelle

A look at the class as a whole (Figure 2.2) shows some students who are able to stay focused and engaged with their reading for the entire time (Rebecca, Tripp, Alice, Isabelle). Quite a few students, on the other hand, have trouble getting settled right away and are distracted or working to get set up for the entire first ten minutes (Mason, Allan, Pete, Jose, Selma). Still others seem to be engaged at the start, but then start to fizzle out by the end (Allessandra, Desiree).

Marelle, a focused, quiet girl, spends much of her reading workshop time reading after taking about five minutes to set up. She switches books frequently, but never in the midst of a book. This shows she is able to continue reading from book to book, staying engaged the entire workshop period. At one point in the workshop (around 10:10 A.M.) she begins smiling, demonstrating engagement through an emotional response to her book.

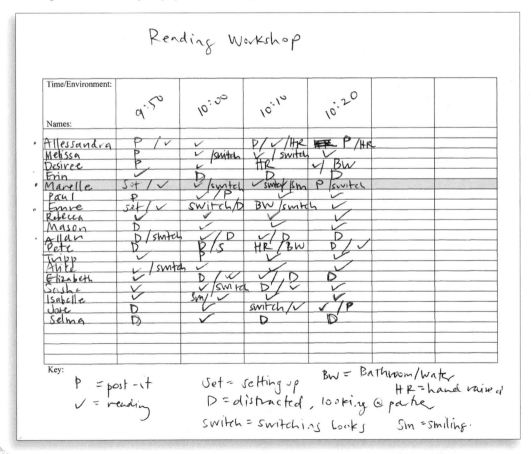

Figure 2.2 Marelle's Engagement Inventory

How I'd Summarize My Findings

Here is how I might summarize my conclusions about Marelle based on the engagement inventory:

Tool	Strengths	Possibilities for Growth
Engagement inventory— reading workshop	• Has strategies to set herself up for a successful reading period • Can sustain reading for long periods of time • Smiles in response to her reading	• Shorten setup time to maximize independent reading

Excerpt from main table on pages 97–99

Using the Book Log

Book logs can give information about reading rate as well as book choice. But to fully mine their potential as an assessment tool, I encourage you to read between the lines, to suss out what these logs are communicating about a child's identity as a reader.

If you're using a rereading log, which I recommended in Chapter 1 for children reading at mid-K through mid-first-grade reading levels, you can learn about the types of books, authors, and or genres that a child chooses to return to again and again and which ones the child chooses to never return to, after reading it only once. You can learn about the total number of books a child reads in school each day and the number of books at home. From that, you can deduce whether a child's engagement is consistent from one place to the other. You could also calculate the average number of words per book based on the level against the total number of books read in a week and divide that by the number of minutes of reading time at home and at school to get a sense of the child's overall reading volume. This last piece of information is about the only thing you can glean from the tally log.

When looking at emergent readers at the beginning of kindergarten, you'll often find that your observations of them, rather than a log, will give you the most insight into their engagement. For example, you may want to look to see if they can sustain attention in one book. Teaching them to tell the story back instead of just flipping through pages quickly glancing at the pictures will develop their sense of story and help them to stay engaged for longer periods of time.

For logs where students record author, title, and pages and minutes read, which I'd recommend for kids who read at late first- through second-grade levels, you can dig a little deeper. Is a student jumping into a reading life with both feet? What does the reading rate tell you about his appetite for reading? When you examine the child's book choices, what's your take? Avid reader or a bit of "autopilot" behavior going on? For example, I taught a child who plowed through just about every book in a popular series at a decent pace, but when I paused to consider it was March and she hadn't veered into other authors and genres, suddenly her reading engagement didn't seem as robust to me.

Looking at Logs to Determine Reading Rate

In late kindergarten, and first and second grade, you may want to calculate *word-per-minute* rate where the only information you have from a log is the total number of books read. This word-per-minute rate can help you estimate the approximate number of books a child should be expected to read in a workshop period. See the table in Figure 2.3 for more information. Keep in mind that these rates are based on *oral* reading, not silent reading, and that there is a range in book length and recommended rates.

Expectations for Reading Volume Based on Words-per-Minute Rate

Reading Level	Approximate Number of Words per Book	Expected WPM Rate (Harris and Sipay 1990)	Expected WPM Rate (Fountas and Pinnell 2008)	Approximate Total # of Books to Read in 30 Minutes
J/K (end of 1st)	850–2,000	60–90	75–100	2–3 books
M (end of 2nd)	5,000–11,000	85–120	90–120	¼–½ a book

Figure 2.3

Looking closely at the logs students might use at level J and above, where they record the author, title, pages, and minutes read, will help you to discover a lot. You can learn the types of books that seem to be appealing to the reader and which of these the reader has success with. By looking across the titles the student has read, you can discover if there is a particular author, series, or genre that she tends to gravitate toward. By comparing the titles with the reading rates, you can see if there are certain titles that seem to slow the reader down, perhaps indicating a lessened sense of engagement with the book. (Of course, it could also be the case that the student is simply slowing down to savor every word.)

Some prefer to calculate a *page-per-minute* rate once children read chapter books. In general, readers of fictional chapter books should read at a rate of about three-quarters of a page per minute silently. Although it may seem strange that a child reading the Cam Jansen series (Adler) should read at the same page per minute rate as someone reading *Maniac Magee* (Spinelli 1999), the truth is that they *aren't* reading at the same rate. Because word-per-minute rate should increase as readers read higher levels, and along with that increased word-per-minute rate, the density of print on a page becomes greater. In the end, it all works out to be about three-quarters of a page per minute. Reading rate is harder to estimate when reading informational texts because print size, layout, and text features vary greatly within a level.

An interesting comparison can be to look at the child's reading rate (or total volume of reading) at school versus at home. Or, when the student reads in the morning in school versus in the afternoon in school. For some readers, there may be a time of day or even a location that lends itself to more engaged reading.

What to Look For

It's helpful to have more than one week's worth of logs on hand so that you can look for trends over time. It may also be the case that the answers to these questions actually bring up more questions that you'd want to discuss with the student. For example, if you notice a good reading rate at home but not a great one in school, you might question whether the place the child sits is the best for him, or if there are particular distractions in school. Having this conversation with a student might give more definitive answers than just your examination of the log will.

Book Log Look-Fors

Question to Ask	Where to Look	The Ideal
What is the child's page-per-minute (PPM) rate or word-per-minute (WPM) rate in school? At home? In the afternoon? In the morning?	For PPM, first, subtract the start and end times. Then, subtract the start and end pages. Divide the number of pages by the number of minutes. For WPM, calculate the total number of pages in a book multiplied by the total number of books read divided by the number of minutes.	PPM: ¾, or .75, regardless of time or location. WPM: See page 41 for level-specific ranges.
Are there certain books that the student seems to be more successful with (as evidenced by a good PPM/WPM rate or as evidenced by a child returning to those books by choice if rereading)?	Compare the PPM/WPM rate of some types of books (genre, author, series) against others.	A better rate or choosing to reread certain types of books can help you steer a student toward other books with which she's likely to be successful.
Are there certain books that this student seems to gravitate toward? Does the student vary authors, genres, and/or series?	Look in the title and author columns. Do you notice a pattern (i.e., similar genre? same author? same series?) or, if examining a rereading log, look to see which books the student chooses to reread the most.	It's a good idea for students to accomplish balance in her reading "diet." However, a child aware of her own tastes as a reader as evidenced by a clear pattern, is also positive.
Does the student read books at an appropriate level?	If your log has one, look at the level column. Otherwise, jot the level of each title along the margin.	The student reads books she'll be successful with—at or slightly below her independent level.

continues

Book Log Look-Fors (cont.)

Question to Ask	Where to Look	The Ideal
Does the student finish a book before starting a new one (level J and above log only)?	Look at the last entry for a given book. Look to see if the last page number listed is the last page of the book.	Most students are better able to comprehend when they finish one book before starting another. There is a tendency to confuse details when multiple books are read simultaneously. Therefore, it's a sign of good reading habits to read and finish one book before starting another.

A Sample Analysis: Marelle

Marelle's classroom teacher does not ask students to keep a log. Because Marelle seems engaged when I look at her engagement inventory, and because I watched her finish a book, put it away, and take out another four times, I would assume that a rereading log would show us that she read five level F books within the thirty minutes allotted for independent reading. Therefore, her overall reading volume seems OK.

Using the Reading Interest Inventory

The reading interest inventory will give you information about a student's self-awareness about reading habits, interests, and attitudes. As mentioned in Chapter 1, you can do this inventory orally for kindergarteners and first graders or in written form for second graders.

As you look at a student's reading interest inventory, notice not only what the student says about *reading*, but also what the student says about interests in general that may be applicable to reading. For example, favorite TV shows might help you make book recommendations based on topics or themes.

What to Look For

What you'll get from the inventory depends on what you've asked and how you've asked it. Open-ended questions are best because they often lead to more honest answers. You can also always ask a student follow-up questions or ask him to elaborate, during a conference. Here are some predictable questions I'll ask myself when analyzing a reading interest inventory:

Reading Interest Inventory Look-Fors

Question to Ask	Where to Look	The Ideal
Does the student seem to have generally positive or negative feelings about reading?	Answers to questions such as "How do you feel about reading?"	I hope for honesty and an ability to self-reflect, less that a student has all warm and fuzzy memories. Knowing about a student's negative and positive experiences will help you create the best circumstances possible for him this year.
Is the student able to name a genre, author, or type of book that is a "good fit"?	Answers to questions such as "What kinds of books do you like to read?" and "Do you have a favorite author or series?"	Again, I'd hope for the ability to self-reflect and that the student has some positive association with some type of author, series, or genre. It is also nice to see when a student has interests in more than one area.
How do the student's interests outside of reading match up with the child's interests in regard to reading?	Compare answers to questions about reading interests (topics, genres) to questions such as "What do you like to do at home and on the weekends?" or "What kind of TV shows/movies do you like?"	Ideally, there is overlap here. (When working with a student who is having trouble engaging, a mismatch here could signal that the student needs support with book choice.)
Does the student seem to have an outside-of-school support network to encourage reading?	Answers to questions such as "Who reads with you at home?" or "With whom do you like to talk about the books you read?"	Ideally, the student finds some pleasure in interacting with others around texts—a family member or peer.

continues

Reading Interest Inventory Look-Fors (cont.)

Question to Ask	Where to Look	The Ideal
What reading habits and stamina does the child report?	Answers to questions such as "How much time do you spend reading each day?" and "How often do you read?" and "When you read, do you concentrate or do you get distracted?"	The child reads each day in school and every night, even when not assigned.* The student should have strategies for staying focused and a reading "spot" that works for her.

*At the beginning of kindergarten, before children are reading conventionally, they may take some reading material home and spend time with the books. This may be them retelling a familiar story to themselves as they turn the pages and/or pointing at and labeling what they see in the pictures. It is also important to note if they are spending some time each day at home being read to by a family member.

A Sample Analysis: Marelle

Marelle seems to have generally positive feelings about reading, describing it as "fun" (Figure 2.4). She seems to know some types of books that she likes and the types of TV shows she prefers; she seems to enjoy stories. Also positive is that she knows that she likes to read in a quiet, distraction-free location where others don't bother her. The fact that she reads independently at home shows she has developed some good habits around reading.

The one concerning piece from her responses it that it seems like she's overly concerned with levels and with the print-based challenges of reading. She seems to have an understanding that reading is learning words, rather than enjoying a story. She describes her reading process as "trying very hard books that you can still read." I wonder if a focus on more of the meaning and comprehension would help round out Marelle's concept of what it means to be a reader.

> Marelle
>
> Felings about reading?
>
> Fun. I like reading 4c I can learn some words that are very hard. You have levels you could read +some are very hard but you can still read, Gotta try to be the letters.
>
> where do you like to read?
>
> Where it's quiet. In my bedroom. Nobody comes in.
>
> Anyone read to you?
>
> No. My mom sometimes.
>
> Kind?
>
> Stories. About fashion.
>
> TV?
>
> Different kinds. Disney XD. Movies. Epic.
>
> Do outside of school?
>
> Play @ playground. I go to piano on wednesday.

Figure 2.4 Marelle's May Reading Interest Inventory

How I'd Summarize My Findings

Tool	Strengths	Possibilities for Growth
Reading interest inventory	• Finds a place to read that works for her • Knows what kinds of books she enjoys	• Expand her definition of reading as more than about reading the "hard words" • Support her making meaning and understanding the story

Excerpt from main table on pages 97–99

ACTION →

Take out the artifact(s) that will help you understand your student's level of reading engagement. If you're trying out this protocol with Emre's work, you should be looking at the engagement inventory (page 159) and the reading interest inventory (page 160). After you do your own evaluation, you can see some of my thinking by turning to Appendix A.

Analyzing Writing About Reading: Short Text Thinking Record, Read-Aloud Stop-and-Jots, Reading Notebooks

In the 1980s, reading comprehension studies examined the thinking of proficient readers to determine what it is that they do when they read. Researchers were able to distill comprehension down to seven aspects (Duffy et. al 1987; Paris, Cross, and Lipson 1984; Keene and Zimmermann 2007; Harvey and Goudvis 2007). The seven mentioned also in Chapter 1, are:

- activating relevant prior knowledge
- determining the most important ideas and themes in a text
- creating visual and other sensory images from the text during and after reading
- drawing inferences from the text
- retelling or synthesizing

- asking questions
- utilizing a variety of fix-up strategies to repair comprehension when it breaks down

Some have suggested that these thinking strategies, or what I'll refer to as "skills," should become the reading curriculum in grades K–8 (Pearson, Roehler, Dole, and Duffy 1992). To some curriculum developers, this means that students work inside of units of study where each unit explores one strategy in-depth (Harvey and Goudvis 2007). Others have argued that students need to use these strategies in concert, when applicable, and instead suggest that units of study are best crafted around genres or purposes for reading, with multiple reading strategies being utilized across the month (Calkins 2013).

Either way, because of the popularization of reading workshop where students read self-selected independent-level texts, these seven skills have been an important foundation for reading instruction.

Now, with the advent of the Common Core State Standards (CCSS 2010), a deep level of comprehension is expected of all students. Look at the Reading Literature Standards and Reading Information Standards for a portrait of the types of understanding, analysis, comparison, and insight that are expected. Although the following is by no means exhaustive, in first grade, these standards articulate some of what students are expected to do:

- retell stories, including key details, and demonstrate understanding of their central message or lesson (RL 1.2)
- compare and contrast the adventures and experiences of characters in stories (RL 1.9)
- describe the connection between two individuals, events, ideas, or pieces of information in a text (RI 1.3)
- use the illustrations and details in a text to describe its key details (RI 1.7)
- interpret theme (RL 4.2)

What to Look For

Although the seven comprehension skills offer us a helpful framework for examining student's thinking, understanding if students are getting the most from their reading isn't as simple as a seven-item checklist. It's important, then, that you aren't looking simply at evidence for or absence of skills. Instead, it's important to consider how deep a student's work reaches within a particular skill.

You might, for example, ask students to respond to prompts you've prepared during a read-aloud. Because all students are responding to the same book at an identical spot, it will be easy for you to compare their answers. You can sort their responses to the same question in piles. Responses that seem basic will go in one pile, those that feel on-target will go in a second pile, and those that are especially sophisticated will go in a third pile. These piles will give you a sense of how a child's work *within a skill* could become deeper and deeper (Serravallo 2010).

For example, I recently asked a second-grade class to stop and jot in response to the question "What kind of person is Jeremy?" while reading from *Those Shoes* by Maribeth Boelts (2009). The story is about a young boy who lives with his grandma in a city. Everyone in his school has the cool new sneakers—the black high-tops with two white stripes. We learn that Jeremy's grandma can't afford to buy them for him. Determined, he shops thrift shops until he finds some they can afford, but they are too small for him. He buys them anyway with his own money. Later in the story, he gives the shoes away to Antonio, a boy who really needs new shoes when his fall apart.

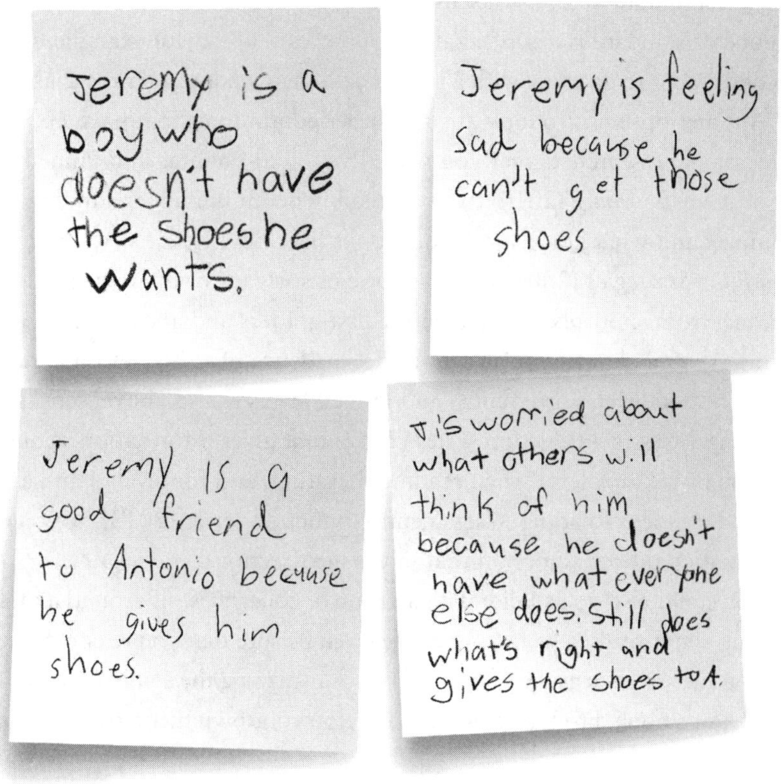

Figure 2.5 Sample Student Responses from Four Different Second Graders Who Stopped and Jotted While Reading *Those Shoes* by Maribeth Boelts

Jeremy is a boy who doesn't have the shoes he wants.

Jeremy is feeling sad because he can't get those shoes

Jeremy is a good friend to Antonio because he gives him shoes.

J is worried about what others will think of him because he doesn't have what everyone else does. Still does what's right and gives the shoes to A.

Sample student responses to the question, "What kind of person is Jeremy?" appear in Figure 2.5. You might notice that in the most basic of the responses, the student simply names some facts that we know about Jeremy from what the author tells us in the words and what the illustrator shows us in the pictures. In a slightly more sophisticated response, the student infers some of what Jeremy might be feeling. An even more sophisticated response names character traits, and the strongest response thinks about Jeremy with a bit more complexity.

Although it is tempting for me to break down each and every reading skill into some theoretical learning progression, naming the qualities of basic to sophisticated thinking, the truth is that it's a bit more complicated than that. What would be considered a sophisticated response for a kindergartener is not the same thing as what would be considered a sophisticated response for a second grader. What is considered a basic response for a child reading *Sheep in a Jeep* (Shaw 1997) is not the same as what would be considered a basic response for a child reading the Amber Brown series (Danziger).

So, what's a teacher to do? There are a few options that will help you start to develop a frame of mind for thinking in this way. One is the CCSS. These standards can serve as a rough continuum to give us a sense of what to expect, by year's end, at each grade level. Each numbered standard is described along a progression—so, for example, standard 2.2 asks a second grader to do more with a similar skill than what standard 1.2 asks of a first grader.

Another option is to look at some other continuums that have been published by educational researchers that you trust. I've found Fountas and Pinnell's *The Continuum of Literacy Learning* (2010) to be incredibly helpful in understanding how texts get more complex and what grade-level work looks like. Ellin Keene's *Assessing Comprehension Thinking Strategies* (2006) gives a rubric of sorts for evaluating students' writing about reading from short texts, intended for first graders and above. Like a continuum, she names several "levels" for how to notice evidence of strategies on a more basic to most sophisticated level. For Fountas and Pinnell levels K and above, see also my Independent Reading Assessment: Fiction series (2012) that gives information about what to expect of readers by reading level when reading literature, and for levels J and above, the companion Independent Reading Assessment: Nonfiction series (2013), which does the same for informational texts (more on that in the next section).

You could also do as I did: with a group of colleagues, sit around a table and sort student writing about reading from your grade level. Be sure that you're comparing apples to apples: look at the students at the same grade level answering the same question from the same spot in the same book. From this, you can develop your own theoretical learning progressions.

Writing about Reading Look-Fors

Question to Ask	Where to Look	The Ideal
What reading skill(s) does the student tend to use?	Look across several days' worth of reading responses, or stop-and-jots on sticky notes.	The student uses a balance of skills when approaching a text. The student doesn't simply use a skill when it's mentioned in the day's minilesson, but instead the student knows when to use a skill to enhance his understanding of a text.
How deep is the work the student is doing?	Look at a couple of samples of work where the student uses the same skill (i.e., inferring).	Compare the student's work against a standard you trust for the given grade level and/or level of text complexity, for example, the Independent Reading Assessment series (Serravallo 2012, 2013) or Fountas and Pinnell's *The Continuum of Literacy Learning* (2010), or the CCSS.

A Sample Analysis: Marelle

The two pages of writing about reading from Marelle's reading notebook (Figure 2.6), the stop-and-jot during a read-aloud (Figure 2.7), and the stop-and-jot during her independent reading (Figure 2.8) show similar proficiencies. Marelle seems to understand the plot in her stories. In all three examples, she uses the words *I think* to begin her jot, but she is actually reiterating information that is quite clear from reading the text. When she writes an entire entry, she arrives at a somewhat simple idea ("Miss Milly is *funny*"). When responding during a read-aloud, she says that Jeremy is "kind," but the evidence she provides ("He doesn't want the shoes") doesn't quite match with her idea. I think that Marelle could use some more support with inferring and learning about the difference between what the text says and what she *thinks* about what the text says.

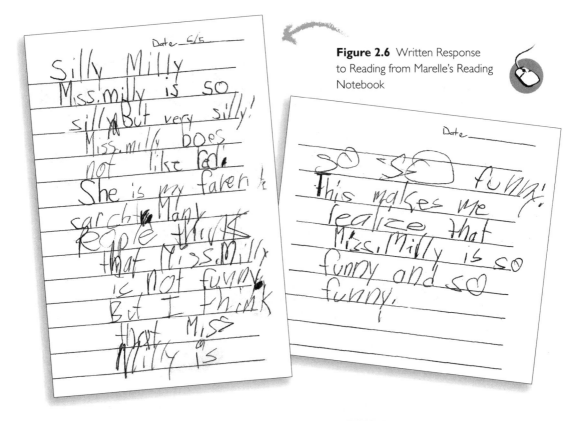

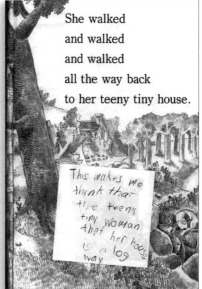

Date __5/5__

Silly Milly
Miss.milly is so
silly But very silly!
Miss.milly Does
not like Red.
She is my faveriht
carch. Many
people think
that Miss.milly
is not funny.
But I think
that Miss
Milly is

Figure 2.6 Written Response to Reading from Marelle's Reading Notebook

Date _____

so so funny!
This makes me
realize that
Miss.Milly is so
funny and so
funny.

Figure 2.7 One of Marelle's Stop-and-Jots during a Whole-Class Read-Aloud

I think that Jarmy
Does not wont
thoes shoes
because it
does not fite on
him. This makes
me thingk

tha Jarmy is
kind.

She walked
and walked
and walked
all the way back
to her teeny tiny house.

This makes me think that the teeny tiny woman that her hoose is a log way

Figure 2.8 An Example of Marelle's Writing about Reading during Independent Reading

How I'd Summarize My Findings

To summarize my conclusions from Marelle's writing about reading, I'd write:

Tool	Strengths	Possibilities for Growth
Writing about reading	• Rephrases what happens in the story • Has a simple idea about a character ("funny")	• Infer further beyond the story
		Excerpt from main table on pages 97–99

Evaluating Responses to a Whole-Book Comprehension Assessment

By the time readers get to chapter books, around the beginning to middle of second grade, running records begin to be less helpful in diagnosing instructional next steps. At lower levels, teachers need to look closely at student miscues and fluency, which oral reading records allow them to do. However, chapter books and whole informational texts offer an array of unique comprehension challenges, asking readers to synthesize between and across chapters and sections. For example, students need to understand not only the plot and characters and setting in the moment, but they also need to be able to accumulate information across dozens and eventually hundreds of pages.

Likewise, teachers need to know what to expect of chapter book readers. When conferring with readers in longer books, especially those that are less familiar to the teacher, it's important to have a sense of the ways that leveled chapter books get more complex and to look for *evidence* of students handling these challenges well. Plot and setting, character, vocabulary and figurative language, and themes and ideas all contribute to the complexity of fiction and are lenses through which teachers can assess students' reading proficiencies in fiction. In nonfiction texts, teachers examine students' ability to determine main idea, key details, the meaning of vocabulary, and information from text features to assess students' facility with nonfiction. (See Serravallo's Independent Reading Assessment for Fiction series [2012] and Independent Reading Assessment for Nonfiction series [2013].)

Whatever tool you decide to use, I strongly encourage you to consider the value of understanding how your students are handling the complexities of the given level they are reading and to keep an eye on how well students are accumulating and synthesizing longer swathes of text. See Figures 2.9 through 2.16 for a summarized view of ways that expectations for readers should increase as the text gets more complex (from the Independent Reading Assessment series [Serravallo 2012, 2013]).

Increasing Expectations for Comprehension in Literature

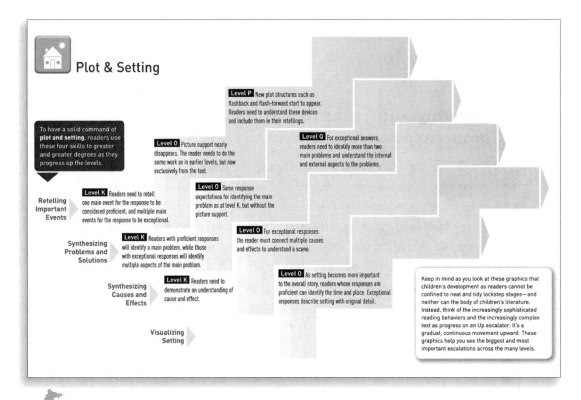

Figure 2.9
Excerpt from Increasing Expectations for Understanding Plot and Setting as Texts Become More Complex

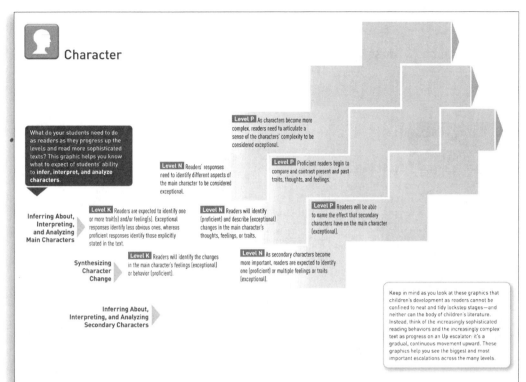

Character

What do your students need to do as readers as they progress up the levels and read more sophisticated texts? This graphic helps you know what to expect of students' ability to **infer, interpret, and analyze characters.**

Inferring About, Interpreting, and Analyzing Main Characters

Level K Readers are expected to identify one or more trait(s) and/or feeling(s). Exceptional responses identify less obvious ones, whereas proficient responses identify those explicitly stated in the text.

Level N Readers' responses need to identify different aspects of the main character to be considered exceptional.

Level P As characters become more complex, readers need to articulate a sense of the characters' complexity to be considered exceptional.

Level P Proficient readers begin to compare and contrast present and past traits, thoughts, and feelings.

Level N Readers will identify (proficient) and describe (exceptional) changes in the main character's thoughts, feelings, or traits.

Level P Readers will be able to name the effect that secondary characters have on the main character (exceptional).

Synthesizing Character Change

Level K Readers will identify the changes in the main character's feelings (exceptional) or behavior (proficient).

Level N As secondary characters become more important, readers are expected to identify one (proficient) or multiple feelings or traits (exceptional).

Inferring About, Interpreting, and Analyzing Secondary Characters

Keep in mind as you look at these graphics that children's development as readers cannot be confined to neat and tidy lockstep stages—and neither can the body of children's literature. Instead, think of the increasingly sophisticated reading behaviors and the increasingly complex text as progress on an Up escalator: it's a gradual, continuous movement upward. These graphics help you see the biggest and most important escalations across the many levels.

Figure 2.10
Excerpt from Increasing Expectations for Understanding Character as Texts Become More Complex

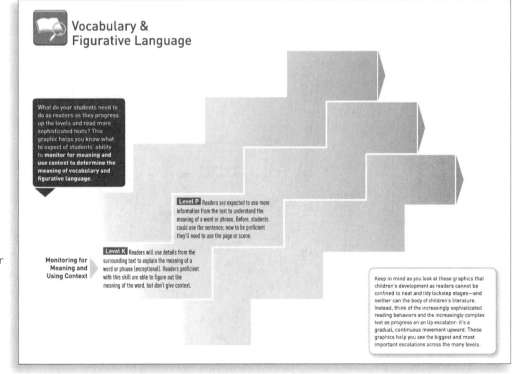

Vocabulary & Figurative Language

What do your students need to do as readers as they progress up the levels and read more sophisticated texts? This graphic helps you know what to expect of students' ability to **monitor for meaning and use context to determine the meaning of vocabulary and figurative language.**

Level P Readers are expected to use more information from the text to understand the meaning of a word or phrase. Before, students could use the sentence; now to be proficient they'll need to use the page or scene.

Monitoring for Meaning and Using Context

Level K Readers will use details from the surrounding text to explain the meaning of a word or phrase (exceptional). Readers proficient with this skill are able to figure out the meaning of the word, but don't give context.

Keep in mind as you look at these graphics that children's development as readers cannot be confined to neat and tidy lockstep stages—and neither can the body of children's literature. Instead, think of the increasingly sophisticated reading behaviors and the increasingly complex text as progress on an Up escalator: it's a gradual, continuous movement upward. These graphics help you see the biggest and most important escalations across the many levels.

Figure 2.11
Excerpt from Increasing Expectations for Understanding Vocabulary and Figurative Language as Texts Become More Complex

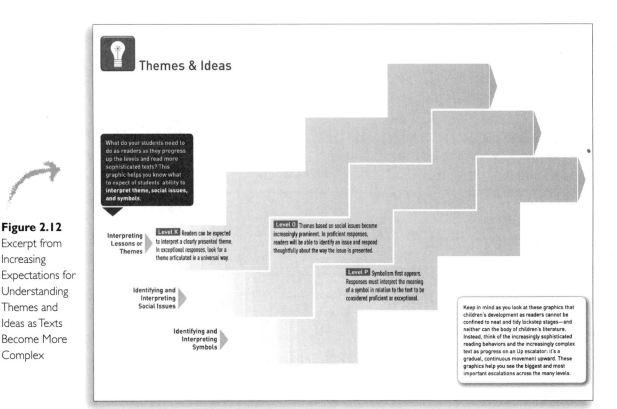

Figure 2.12
Excerpt from Increasing Expectations for Understanding Themes and Ideas as Texts Become More Complex

Themes & Ideas

What do your students need to do as readers as they progress up the levels and read more sophisticated texts? This graphic helps you know what to expect of students' ability to **interpret theme, social issues, and symbols.**

Interpreting Lessons or Themes

Level K Readers can be expected to interpret a clearly presented theme. In exceptional responses, look for a theme articulated in a universal way.

Level O Themes based on social issues become increasingly prominent. In proficient responses, readers will be able to identify an issue and respond thoughtfully about the way the issue is presented.

Identifying and Interpreting Social Issues

Level P Symbolism first appears. Responses must interpret the meaning of a symbol in relation to the text to be considered proficient or exceptional.

Identifying and Interpreting Symbols

Keep in mind as you look at these graphics that children's development as readers cannot be confined to neat and tidy lockstep stages—and neither can the body of children's literature. Instead, think of the increasingly sophisticated reading behaviors and the increasingly complex text as progress on an Up escalator: it's a gradual, continuous movement upward. These graphics help you see the biggest and most important escalations across the many levels.

Increasing Expectations for Comprehension of Informational Texts

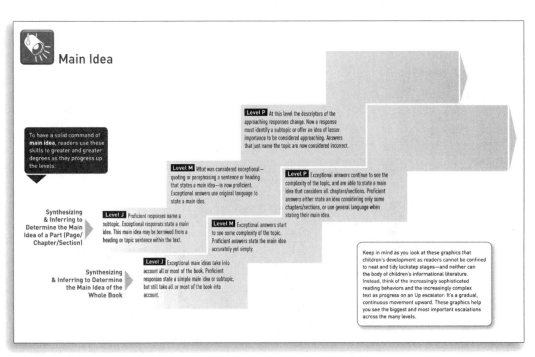

Main Idea

To have a solid command of **main idea**, readers use these skills to greater and greater degrees as they progress up the levels.

Level P At this level the descriptors of the approaching responses change. Now a response must identify a subtopic or offer an idea of lesser importance to be considered approaching. Answers that just name the topic are now considered incorrect.

Level M What was considered exceptional—quoting or paraphrasing a sentence or heading that states a main idea—is now proficient. Exceptional answers use original language to state a main idea.

Level P Exceptional answers continue to see the complexity of the topic, and are able to state a main idea that considers all chapters/sections. Proficient answers either state an idea considering only some chapters/sections, or use general language when stating their main idea.

Synthesizing & Inferring to Determine the Main Idea of a Part (Page/ Chapter/Section)

Level J Proficient responses name a subtopic. Exceptional responses state a main idea. This main idea may be borrowed from a heading or topic sentence within the text.

Level M Exceptional answers start to see some complexity of the topic. Proficient answers state the main idea accurately yet simply.

Synthesizing & Inferring to Determine the Main Idea of the Whole Book

Level J Exceptional main ideas take into account all or most of the book. Proficient responses state a simple main idea or subtopic, but still take all or most of the book into account.

Keep in mind as you look at these graphics that children's development as readers cannot be confined to neat and tidy lockstep stages—and neither can the body of children's informational literature. Instead, think of the increasingly sophisticated reading behaviors and the increasingly complex text as progress on an Up escalator: It's a gradual, continuous movement upward. These graphics help you see the biggest and most important escalations across the many levels.

Figure 2.13
Excerpt from Increasing Expectations for Understanding Main Idea as Texts Become More Complex

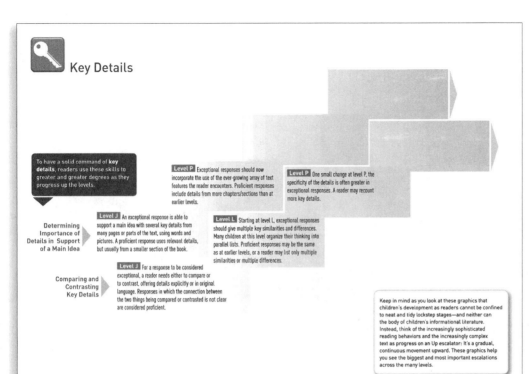

Key Details

To have a solid command of **key details**, readers use these skills to greater and greater degrees as they progress up the levels.

Determining Importance of Details in Support of a Main Idea

Level J An exceptional response is able to support a main idea with several key details from many pages or parts of the text, using words and pictures. A proficient response uses relevant details, but usually from a smaller section of the book.

Comparing and Contrasting Key Details

Level J For a response to be considered exceptional, a reader needs either to compare or to contrast, offering details explicitly or in original language. Responses in which the connection between the two things being compared or contrasted is not clear are considered proficient.

Level P Exceptional responses should now incorporate the use of the ever-growing array of text features the reader encounters. Proficient responses include details from more chapters/sections than at earlier levels.

Level L Starting at level L, exceptional responses should give multiple key similarities and differences. Many children at this level organize their thinking into parallel lists. Proficient responses may be the same as at earlier levels, or a reader may list only multiple similarities or multiple differences.

Level P One small change at level P, the specificity of the details is often greater in exceptional responses. A reader may recount more key details.

Keep in mind as you look at these graphics that children's development as readers cannot be confined to neat and tidy lockstep stages—and neither can the body of children's informational literature. Instead, think of the increasingly sophisticated reading behaviors and the increasingly complex text as progress on an Up escalator: It's a gradual, continuous movement upward. These graphics help you see the biggest and most important escalations across the many levels.

Figure 2.14
Excerpt from Increasing Expectations for Understanding Key Details as Texts Become More Complex

Figure 2.15
Excerpt from Increasing Expectations for Understanding Vocabulary as Texts Become More Complex

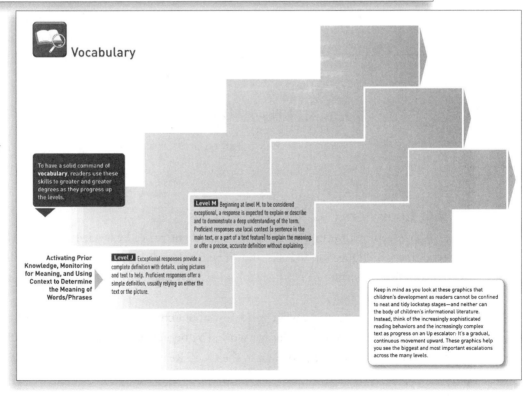

Vocabulary

To have a solid command of **vocabulary**, readers use these skills to greater and greater degrees as they progress up the levels.

Activating Prior Knowledge, Monitoring for Meaning, and Using Context to Determine the Meaning of Words/Phrases

Level J Exceptional responses provide a complete definition with details, using pictures and text to help. Proficient responses offer a simple definition, usually relying on either the text or the picture.

Level M Beginning at level M, to be considered exceptional, a response is expected to explain or describe and to demonstrate a deep understanding of the term. Proficient responses use local context (a sentence in the main text, or a part of a text feature) to explain the meaning, or offer a precise, accurate definition without explaining.

Keep in mind as you look at these graphics that children's development as readers cannot be confined to neat and tidy lockstep stages—and neither can the body of children's informational literature. Instead, think of the increasingly sophisticated reading behaviors and the increasingly complex text as progress on an Up escalator: It's a gradual, continuous movement upward. These graphics help you see the biggest and most important escalations across the many levels.

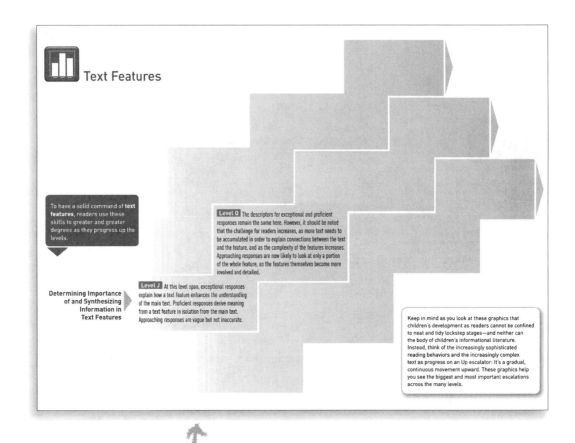

Text Features

To have a solid command of **text features**, readers use these skills to greater and greater degrees as they progress up the levels.

Level Q The descriptors for exceptional and proficient responses remain the same here. However, it should be noted that the challenge for readers increases, as more text needs to be accumulated in order to explain connections between the text and the feature, and as the complexity of the features increases. Approaching responses are now likely to look at only a portion of the whole feature, as the features themselves become more involved and detailed.

Determining Importance of and Synthesizing Information in Text Features

Level J At this level span, exceptional responses explain how a text feature enhances the understanding of the main text. Proficient responses derive meaning from a text feature in isolation from the main text. Approaching responses are vague but not inaccurate.

Keep in mind as you look at these graphics that children's development as readers cannot be confined to neat and tidy lockstep stages—and neither can the body of children's informational literature. Instead, think of the increasingly sophisticated reading behaviors and the increasingly complex text as progress on an Up escalator: It's a gradual, continuous movement upward. These graphics help you see the biggest and most important escalations across the many levels.

Figure 2.16 Excerpt from Increasing Expectations for Understanding Text Features as Texts Become More Complex

What to Look For

What you'll be looking for in a whole-book assessment varies by level. Therefore, what you see in both the "Question to Ask" and "The Ideal" columns in the chart that follows is what would be important to consider for an average end-of-first-grade reader, reading level J informational texts.

Of course, you'll want to use what you know about characteristics of the level of books of your focus student as you consider her work. I've organized the questions—what to look for—in four strands that also align to the CCSS Reading Information standards:

Whole-Book Comprehension Look-Fors (Level J, Informational Texts)

Question to Ask	Where to Look	The Ideal
Main idea (CCSS RI 1.2, 1.7)*	Answers to questions such as "What is this section mostly about?" or "What is the main idea of this whole book?"	Because the main idea is often stated explicitly at the start of each new section/page spread at this level, the reader should be able to quote or paraphrase the main idea. When asked about the main idea of a whole text, the reader should take most or all of the book into account and be able to state a simple main idea.
Key details (CCSS RI 1.1, 1.2, 1.7)	Answers to questions such as "What details support the main idea that ____?" or "What details support the main idea you just wrote?" or "Compare or contrast ____ and ____."	The reader should be able to select key details that fit with the main idea, drawing information from text and/or pictures. When asked to compare/contrast, the reader should be able to state at least one thing that's the same or one that's different, drawing information from text and/or pictures.
Vocabulary (CCRI 1.4)	Answers to questions such as "What does ____ mean?" or "Explain what ____ means."	The reader should be able to state a complete definition with some detail from the text and/or pictures.
Text features (CCRI 1.5, 1.6)	Answers to questions such as "What can you learn from the (photo/caption/glossary) on page ____?" or "How does what you learn in the picture fit with what you're learning on this page?"	The reader should be able to explain how a text feature adds to, or connects with, the meaning in a text.

*It will be important to look to your grade-specific standards because expectations for thinking are closely aligned to complexity in the text.

A Sample Analysis: Marelle

Because Marelle is currently reading at a level F and the Independent Reading Assessment begins at level J for nonfiction and K for fiction, this whole-book independent reading assessment isn't a good choice for her. There is an example of this type of assessment and my analysis included in Appendix A, where you'll have a chance to study Emre's work.

ACTION →

Pause here if you haven't already to analyze Emre's work or the work of a student from your class. Take out any work that will help you understand what your reader comprehends. If you're following along with Emre, you should take a look now at his writing about reading from his reader's notebook, his stop-and-jots on sticky notes, his whole-book independent reading assessment for the book *Play Ball* (York), and the comprehension questions on his running record. You can find my thoughts about his work in Appendix A.

Analyzing a Fluency Assessment

An often-overlooked aspect of a running record is that one can also record information about a student's fluency. Often, teachers' attention is solely on recording miscues. But fluency, as many researchers have noted, has direct links to comprehension (Kuhn 2008; Rasinski 2010). In the CCSS document, fluency has its own strand under Reading Foundational Skills (CCSS RF 4). Looking back at a running record with an eye toward fluency, or recording student fluency during an oral reading, and then analyzing it can be helpful.

When looking at a **fluency record** (Figure 2.18), we can gain insight into a student's ability to read with accuracy, expression, and phrasing. Often, these qualities of fluency are necessary precursors to a child's ability to comprehend a text. There are some rare exceptions to instances when this is true. At times, children who have processing or expressive language delays may have a particularly difficult time reading with fluency, although their comprehension is not affected. Likewise, there are some English language learners whose speech is somewhat staccato; expecting more fluency when reading is often not possible.

When studying a child's fluency, it's important to note the role that fluency plays in helping us to match readers to just-right books. In kindergarteners and early first graders reading at levels A–C where one-to-one matching is expected, smooth fluent reading would interfere with acquiring that new skill. Therefore, kids reading at levels A–C will probably read in a way that would match the description of a level 1 on the *National Assessment of Educational Progress* (NAEP) Fluency Scale (see Figure 2.17). Once readers begin reading books at levels D, E, and F, we'd expect increasingly more fluency, with longer phrases and text-appropriate intonation. When readers at levels E and above read at levels 1 or 2 on the NAEP scale, it often indicates that a reader would be better off moving to an easier text. When students are falling somewhere in level 3, but the accuracy and comprehension is high, it's likely that you'll want to set fluency as a potential goal for that student.

NAEP Oral Reading Fluency Scale

Fluent	Level 4	Reads primarily in larger, meaningful phrase groups. Although some regressions, repetitions, and deviations from text may be present, these do not appear to detract from the overall structure of the story. Presentation of the author's syntax is consistent. Some or most of the story is read with expressive interpretation.
	Level 3	Reads primarily in three- or four-word phrase groups. Some small groupings may be present. However, the majority of phrasing seems appropriate and preserves the syntax of the author. Little or no expressive interpretation is present.
Nonfluent	Level 2	Reads primarily in two-word phrases with some three- or four-word groupings. Some word-by-word reading may be present. Word groupings may seem awkward and unrelated to larger context of setting or passage
	Level 1	Reads primarily word-by-word. Occasional two-word or three-word phrases may occur—but these are infrequent and/or they do not preserve meaningful syntax.

Figure 2.17

What to Look For

When analyzing a child's fluency, you can look at a tool like the NAEP fluency scale and/or look for individual qualities of fluent reading. Using the NAEP is more holistic, whereas looking at individual qualities allows you to pinpoint a possible area of need. You might ask:

Fluency Assessment Look-Fors

Question to Ask	Where to Look	The Ideal
How many words are in a phrase, on average?	Count the number of words between each pause ("/") on the record.	Varies by level.* By level E, students should be reading in several word phrases, as on level 2 of the NAEP fluency scale. By reading level F, students' reading should sound more like a level 3 on the NAEP scale.
Where does the reader pause?	Look for a pause or slash ("/") on the record. Between pauses, check to see if the phrase makes sense as a phrase.	Varies by level. By level F, the location of the pauses maintain the author's syntax and preserve meaning.
Does the student attend to punctuation?	Look to see how you noted a child's expression during ending punctuation, such as exclamation points and question marks, and midsentence punctuation such as commas and dashes.	Varies by level. By level F, the student should often use appropriate expression as indicated by punctuation.
Does the student read with expression appropriate to the passage?	Look for any annotations you made about the student's expression.	Varies by level. By level F, when reading dialogue, the expression should match feelings of the character. There should be a difference in how dialogue and narration sounds.
Does the student read words automatically, or does she pause often to figure words out?	Look to see how frequently a pause ("/") precedes a challenging word.	Known words (i.e., high-frequency sight words) should be automatically recognized. Working to figure out a word should happen infrequently.

*Fluency is not expected at early (A–C) levels where children are developing the skill of one-to-one matching. Crisp pointing under words as children speak one word for every word of print on the page is expected. On rereads at level C, and on first reads at level D, students should begin to read in phrases, though those phrases may not be syntactically appropriate.

A Sample Analysis: Marelle

When reading a text at level F, Marelle reads in two- to three-word phrases consistently; sometimes she can read four words before pausing, other times she slips into word-by-word reading. She reads dialogue with some expression. This places her at level 2 on the NAEP fluency scale.

Marelle, who is new to reading books at level F, could benefit from some fluency practice. She reads with a high degree of accuracy, but could work to improve her automaticity and phrasing on rereads.

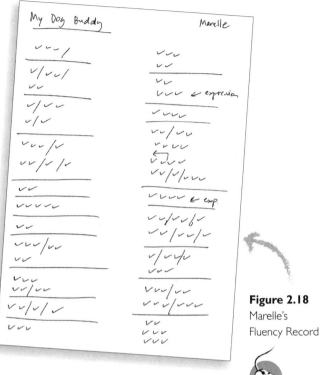

Figure 2.18
Marelle's
Fluency Record

How I'd Summarize My Findings

To summarize my findings about Marelle's fluency, I'd say:

Tool	Strengths	Possibilities for Growth
Fluency (from fluency record)	• 2- to 3-word phrases consistently, some 4-word phrases. • Reads dialogue with expression	• 3- to 4-word phrases consistently, using the natural phrasing (sentence broken across lines) to support her.

Excerpt from main table on pages 97–99

Running Record Miscue Analysis

A running record is a helpful tool to quickly notice a few important aspects of a reader: reading behaviors; the strategies a student uses to figure out unknown words; when and how often a student self-corrects; how fluently a student can read; and whether a student can comprehend a text on a basic level. We've already discussed what to look for in terms of fluency and comprehension; you should apply that knowledge when analyzing a running record. This section will discuss miscue analysis, or analyzing their mistakes, self-corrections, and behaviors to uncover what students do when they encounter unknown words in texts.

I find running records essential for students reading levels A–J. At those levels, having an eye on word-solving strategies is essential. By the time students get to chapter books, a running record might be one tool you use, but it shouldn't be the only one. This is partly because at these levels, the text is longer and a running record would either be an excerpt of a longer text or a text constructed for the purpose of the running record. If kids are reading entire chapter books or informational texts during reading workshop each day, teachers need other ways to keep an eye on comprehension, especially as it pertains to reading a book in its entirety. Whole-book assessments of student comprehension and/or other informal snapshots of a student's thinking in a whole text (such as the read-aloud stop-and-jot assessment described in Chapter 1) are also essential.

Running record miscue analysis is very involved and can be quite complex. Entire books are written about it! In this section, I will offer some basic information to help you get started. However, I encourage you to treat this as merely an introduction and seek out some of the work of Marie Clay, such as her book on running records published by Heinemann in 2000.

You may also consult the CCSS Reading Foundational Skills document, which addresses the sorts of Print Concepts (RF 1) and Phonics and Word Recognition (RF 3) expected by grade level. Of course, many of the types of things we expect students to do in these areas also relate to the level of text at which they are reading. For example, you wouldn't expect a child reading on level C to know the word *because*, even though it is a sight word. Children at level C are more likely to know words such as *and, to, a,* and *my.* To learn what to expect students to be able to do at each level, any of Fountas and Pinnell's materials are good resources (i.e., *Guided Reading* 1996; *Benchmark Assessment System 1* 2010; and so on).

Remember from Chapter 1 that analyzing an instructional-level running record will yield the most information, as there are more opportunities to observe the student's problem-solving behaviors.

What to Look For

When performing a miscue analysis on a running record, make your best inference about what was happening in a student's brain when he is actively working to figure out a word, miscues on a word, or works to self-correct a word. Although it's often hard to be 100% sure about what is going on in a student's brain, we know that readers tend to use three cueing systems: meaning (or semantic information), structure (or syntactical information), and/or visual (graphophonic information).

Using all three cueing systems allows a proficient reader to read a word that matches the meaning of the text, sounds right syntactically, and matches the letters of the word. Students who are learning to read will encounter difficulty in a text and need to work to figure out the word. Their process, and the cueing systems they use, will then become visible.

To analyze a miscue, read up to (but not beyond) the error. Ask yourself three questions to determine if the student used one, two, three, or none of the cueing systems:

- Does the error make sense?
- Does the error sound right?
- Does the error look right?

When students use the *meaning* cueing system, the word they read in error will still make sense with what's happening in the text. A student would need to use knowledge of the story/text so far, as well as any information from the pictures (if there are any). It's possible that the error doesn't mean the same thing as the word in the text, but that you'd still say the student used meaning. For example, if the student reads "I put the *sauce* on my sandwich" and the actual text says "I put the *ketchup* on my sandwich," that error makes sense even though it doesn't mean the exact same thing. Likewise, "I put the *mustard* on my sandwich" makes sense (as long as there isn't a bottle of red stuff in the picture), but doesn't mean the exact same thing.

When students use the *structure* cueing system, the word they read in error sounds syntactically appropriate in the sentence. Often, it's the same part of speech as the word in the text. Both of the examples above—*mustard* or *sauce* instead of *ketchup*—would be syntactically correct because they are nouns. It's possible for a word to not make sense but still be syntactically correct, and vice versa.

When students use the *visual* cueing system, the word they read in error has some of the same letters or sounds in common with the word in the text. Often, as a reader is developing his visual cueing system, he will first pay attention to the initial letter or cluster of letters, next he will be attuned to the end of the word, and attention to the middle of the word usually comes last. *Sauce* and *mustard* do not *look right* because they do not share the same beginning, ending, or middle letters as *ketchup*, the word in the text.

In the instance of a self-correction, you'll want to ask yourself those three questions to analyze the miscue, and then ask yourself those three questions again to analyze the self-correction. In other words, did the student use meaning, syntax, and/or visual to fix his reading of the word?

Once you've analyzed each miscue separately, you'll want to look across the errors to see if you can determine a pattern. I ask myself:

Running Record Look-Fors

Question to Ask	Where to Look	The Ideal
What does the student tend to use when encountering an unknown word?	Look at your analysis of all of the miscues. Count the number of times the student uses meaning, syntax, and visual cueing systems.	The student should use all three cueing systems together. What you might find, however, is a tendency to use one or two of the systems. A student might also use one or two at first, and then "cross-check" using one or two of the others.*
When the student self-corrects, what cueing systems most likely helped him to self-correct?	Look at your analysis of all of the self-corrections. Count the number of times the student uses meaning, syntax, and visual cueing systems to self-correct.	The fact that the student is self-correcting at all is very encouraging. The ideal is a high self-correction rate (that is, almost any time the student makes an error he corrects it). It's interesting to analyze which system the student uses because teaching a student to use this when first encountering a word could help the miscue rate decrease.
What cueing system(s) is the child not using inconsistently?	Look at your analysis of all of the miscues. Count the number of times the student uses meaning, syntax, and visual cueing systems.	Ideally the student uses all three, but if you find that one or two are not being used, then teaching the student to use them together with the most often used cueing system could help to decrease the error rate.

*The first level at which students use all three cueing systems is level C.

I must be careful, as always, to not look for a deficit, but instead for possibility that comes from a strength. One way to do this is to look to see what a child is doing inconsistently that might be helpful for him to do all the time. I look to see what the student's strength is so that I can lean on that strength to support the area of need.

A Sample Analysis: Marelle

When you tally up the cueing systems that Marelle is using when she makes an error, it seems as though she uses meaning often. But actually, that's because she repeatedly reads *we are* instead of *we're* (Figure 2.19).

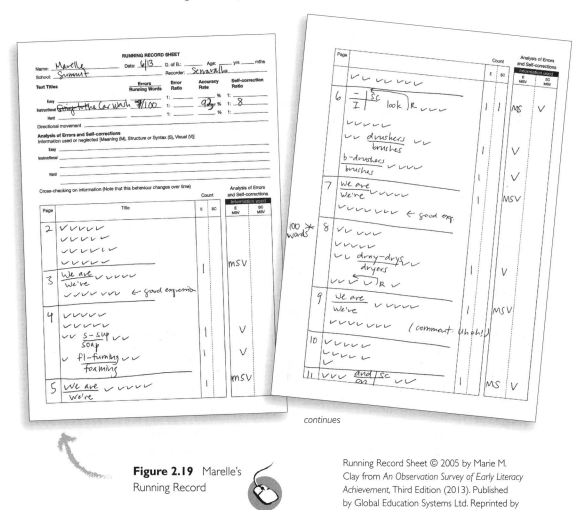

continues

Figure 2.19 Marelle's Running Record

Running Record Sheet © 2005 by Marie M. Clay from *An Observation Survey of Early Literacy Achievement,* Third Edition (2013). Published by Global Education Systems Ltd. Reprinted by permission of the author's estate.

Figure 2.19
continued

Retell:
They went to the car wash 2x.
Theres mud all around.
"Drushers" "splaying" water
The air was drying the car
And it got dirt again.

Questions:
1. Why did they go to the car wash?
     There was mud all around.

2. What are 3 things that happened @ car wash?
     soap, drushes, air.

3. What did the man at the car wash think
     when the car came back?
     That there was more mud! (laughs)

4. How did the people in the car feel @ end?
     Funny. They – the 2 children told
     the man it had dirt all around!

With that miscue aside, she tends to use visual primarily. Often, she is making up a word (*fuming* for *foaming*, *drushers* for *brushes*, *drays* for *dryers*) that might sound syntactically correct as well, but it's hard to be sure because they are not real words. It's possible that because Marelle is an English language learner, she simply doesn't know the vocabulary. In fact, when she answers the second question, "Name three things that happen to the car," she says that one of them is "drushes around." This reinforces the idea that she doesn't know the name of the car wash part, *brushes*.

She self-corrects twice, probably using visual information (once she skips the word *I* and goes back to read it, another time she reads *and* instead of *on* and goes back and fixes it).

How I'd Summarize My Findings

Here is a summary of my conclusions about Marelle's running record:

Tool	Strengths	Possibilities for Growth
Running record	• Uses visual and syntactical cueing systems consistently • Occasionally uses meaning • Retell captures most important information from beginning, middle, and end • Reads sight words automatically • Self-corrects using visual information	• Use meaning consistently • Errors that looked and sounded right but didn't make sense were probably due to lack of vocabulary/background knowledge • Work to self-correct using meaning and/or syntax

Excerpt from main table on pages 97–99

ACTION →

Do an analysis of your student's print work strategies. If you're using Emre's work, take a look at his running record. Analyze miscues as well as fluency. Find out my thinking about his running record in Appendix A.

Analyzing Conversation

When you go back to look at a transcript, listen to a recording, or watch a video of your students' conversation in a book club or partnership, it's helpful to tune in with two lenses in mind. You might be thinking about their abilities to articulate their thinking about the text, *and* you might be thinking about their speaking and listening skills.

Often, it's hard to get everything on just the first look, watch, or listen. That's part of what makes conferring during conversation so difficult—you need to be able to listen, think, and make a decision in the moment. Going back to a recording of the conversation allows you time to revisit the conversation again and again to get all you can from the sample of student work. Looking at a transcript, like the one I have included in this book for Marelle, will allow you to read, process, and think about the student's conversational skills at your own pace.

What to Look For

When looking at a transcript for the first time, or listening to a conversation, it is important to think about the student's abilities in terms of speaking and listening. The CCSS' Speaking and Listening strand has some helpful insights, organized by grade level, about what to expect of students. The Comprehension and Collaboration, Standards 1 and 2, are most helpful for the type of analysis we'll do in this section.

When considering speaking and listening skills, you might ask yourself:

Conversation Look-Fors

Question to Ask	Where to Look	The Ideal
Does the student actively participate in the conversation?	Compare the amount of time each student spends speaking.	There is balance in terms of who is speaking and how much each is saying; in other words, no single student dominates the conversation.
Is the student able to offer ideas that follow the main topic of conversation?	When the student speaks, look to see if what she says relates to what the person before her said.	The student should be able to stay on topic.
Is the student able to build on another student's ideas, deepening the thought, not just repeating the thought?	Compare what the student says to what the person or people before her said. Look to see if it is the same thing in different words.	Ideally the student contributes new or deeper thoughts to the conversation.

continues

Conversation Look-Fors (cont.)

Question to Ask	Where to Look	The Ideal
Does the student use appropriate behaviors during the conversation?	Watch the student's body language during the conversation.	The student should look at the speaker, waiting respectfully for a turn. Natural interjections and interruptions are a great sign of organic conversation, but rudely speaking over others is not.
What does the student do when an idea is offered that differs from his own?	Look for a moment when a member of the conversation offers an idea that differs from the child whose conversation you're evaluating. See what the student does next.	The student should be able to consider another student's ideas. Perhaps the student will try to support the other student's ideas, or she will ask clarifying questions in an effort to better understand where the other student is coming from.
Does the student reference text and/or pictures appropriately during book talks?	Look to see if the student references the text and/or pictures by either opening up the book and reading from it, paraphrasing something from the text, or reading from notes he has written.	The book needs to be in the book talk. Children should be encouraged to discuss details from the text along with their own thoughts and reactions from the text.

The second time you read the transcript or listen to the conversation, you can also think about comprehension. Everything a student says reveals something about his understanding about the text (see Figure 2.20).

- Does the student offer ideas during the conversation that are based on an accurate understanding of the text?
- Which of the reading comprehension skills does the student use, and how deep is the use of each (see section on writing about reading on pages 47–53)?
- How well is the student doing the work of the level (see section on whole-book comprehension, pages 53–60)?

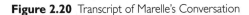

Marelle: [reads two pages from her book]

Partner: What do you think about that character?

Marelle: They don't want to be invited to the fair.

Partner: What makes you think that?

Marelle: Because the girl wants to play with the ball [points to picture, then turns page], and the boy wants to play with the bat [points to picture].

Partner: So what's happening here?

Marelle: They want something else that they can't have.

Partner: So what did you write on this?

Marelle: [reading from sticky note] "This makes me think that the children . . ." Oh. I didn't finish it.

Figure 2.20 Transcript of Marelle's Conversation

A Sample Analysis: Marelle

Marelle feels comfortable during her partnership conversation. She sits side by side with her partner and answers all of her partner's questions. She has the book open on her lap and references the text when speaking. She is also able to stick to one topic for the whole (albeit brief) conversation. She and her partner discuss what the characters want and don't want.

For the conversation to help Marelle's reading skills—which is one of the reasons to set aside time in the classroom for children to talk about books—there needs to be more of a conversation. Perhaps Marelle could not only answer her partner's questions, but could also ask some questions of her partner as well. Also, instead of just talking about what happens in the story, perhaps Marelle could talk about her *ideas about* what happens in the story. Often, it's ideas that are more worth discussing, rather than just the facts of the book, which she seems to understand without any support.

Finally, it seems as though it's a common routine for her and her partner to begin their time together by reading the entire story. If the book is familiar to both of them, another idea is to choose a part to read aloud for some purpose. For example, perhaps she has an idea that a part is funny or surprising. Maybe she could just read the part where she had that thought, and explain why she thought what she did.

How I'd Summarize My Findings

After rereading the transcript of Marelle's conversation with her book club, I'd summarize my interpretations as follows:

Tool	Strengths	Possibilities for Growth
Partnership—reading workshop	• Retells details from her book • Rereads a familiar book with confidence • Sticks to one topic of conversation • Answers questions comfortably	• Give ideas, not just retell • Offer questions to her partner • Choose a part to reread for a purpose

Excerpt from main table on pages 97–99

ACTION →

- Take a look at the notes from one of Emre's partnership conversations or from the conversation of the student you're studying. What do you notice?
- Take a look at any remaining student work or assessments you've collected to better understand your student as a reader, as this concludes the reading section. As you do, consider the type of information you can glean from each piece of work and use the appropriate tables in the preceding sections to help you. If you find that the student work sample you're looking at doesn't actually help you that much to learn about the student, consider eliminating that type of work/assessment from your repertoire. If you're working with Emre's work, you should have analyzed his running record, writing about reading, reading log, and conversation. Remember that you can look at my analysis in Appendix A. If you are analyzing the work of a student reading between levels A and F, you might consider looking at the grade-level-specific tables of behaviors and goals in Appendix D.

◻ Making Discoveries from Narrative Writing

Narrative writing is an umbrella term that incorporates a variety of types of writing. Narrative writing is any type of writing in which a writer attempts to tell a story, with a sequence of events. Narrative writing often has a plot, characters, a setting, and, in the most sophisticated examples, an overarching theme.

To use the advice in this section, you may have in front of you an example of a student's personal narrative, realistic fiction, fantasy, or some other type of genre fiction. Personal narrative is a type of writing in which a writer attempts to tell a story about himself. At the Teachers College Reading and Writing Project, we call a personal narrative that is very focused in time a "small moment" narrative. Young children may attempt to write a story by listing many events linked with "and then" and can be taught to elaborate on those events with dialogue, descriptions of characters, and descriptions of setting. Many writing workshop teachers support students' writing of narrative by having children write across pages in a booklet, each page representing one event in the story.

In the CCSS document, grade-level expectations for narrative writing are under Writing Standard 3. For kindergarten students at an emergent level, look to the first table in Appendix D to see how emergent writing behaviors and goals correlate with emergent reading goals. You can also look to your grade-level standards, or Calkins et al.'s (2013) *Units of Study in Opinion, Information, and Narrative Writing* for kindergarten. For more sophisticated writing behaviors and goals for high-achieving first graders and typically progressing second graders, see your grade-level standards and/or Calkins et al.'s (2013) *Units of Study in Opinion, Information, and Narrative Writing* for second grade.

What to Look For

With any piece of writing, I find it helpful to look at both qualities of good writing and writing process.

I find it most helpful to use the qualities of good writing like a sort of checklist, as I mentioned in the first chapter. Here I'll give you a series of guiding questions underneath each quality of good writing to help focus your analysis. You may also consult the CCSS. They will give you information about what to expect, by grade level, at the end of the year.

Focus refers to the writer's ability to focus a piece in time or by meaning.

For example, a writer with a very broad focus may write a piece about her entire summer vacation. Another might write just about the week at her grandmother's house. One might write about the day they went to Great Adventure, and still another would focus the piece just on the roller-coaster ride. In general, a more focused piece is harder to pull off because the greater the focus, the more the writer will need to elaborate.

When focusing by meaning, a writer must consider "Why am I writing this story?" or "What idea/message/lesson am I trying to communicate?" This type of insight is extremely rare in a young child, however, and when asked what she's trying to show in her story, a child in kindergarten or first or second grade might say something such as "This was fun" or "I was scared."

You'll want to refer to CCSS Writing Standard 3 as one source for grade-level expectations. You may also consult the *Units of Study in Opinion, Information, and Narrative Writing* (Calkins and colleagues 2013) for rubrics aligned to the Common Core. After reading the entire narrative written by an end-of-year first grader, you may ask yourself:

Narrative Writing Look-Fors: Focus

Question to Ask	Where to Look	The Ideal
Is the student able to focus on a moment that is most important?	Notice the beginning, middle, and end of the piece, asking yourself how much time passes during this story.	A child focuses the story by recounting something that lasted during just part of a day.
Does the student maintain the focus in the piece?	Look especially at the beginning and the end, and ask yourself if they relate to each other.	By the end of first grade, children should understand that "I woke up" to start a story and "I went to bed" to end a story is often not needed. Instead, the beginning and ending should pertain to the middle of the story.
How well are details used to support the focus?	Pay attention to different types of details used (dialogue, action, thinking, setting) to see if they match the focus of the story.	At this age, it's more likely that details beyond the main action and some minor dialogue will be added on during revision, without real attention to whether they match the focus of the story.

Structure refers to how a piece is organized. In a first grader's narrative, sequencing is important. Ideally one event will lead to another in a logical way. Once again, you can refer to CCSS Writing 3, or Calkins and colleagues' Units of Study series (2013) for grade-level expectations.

Narrative Writing Look-Fors: Structure

Question to Ask	Where to Look	The Ideal
Is there a sequence of events in the story that makes it easy to follow and understand?	Try to create a timeline from the events of the story. See if one event leads logically to the next.	A reader should be clear on how one event leads to another. Young writers have a tendency to leave events out, assuming the reader possesses the same knowledge about the events as the writer.
How strong is the story's beginning?	Look at the first page (if the student is writing in a booklet) or the first sentences of the story.	The story should start "in the moment," without the common "One day I woke up" or "I was driving in the car" type of lead-ins that don't add to the focus of the story.
Does the story have good closure?	Read the final sentence (or page if the student is writing in a booklet).	The closure should be the very last event that happened while still related to the focus of the story, or should tell the writer's final thoughts or feelings about the moment (i.e., "It was fun").

Elaboration refers to the details in a story. Consider the types of details the writer uses and how well that detail is used. Most young children tend to tell what happens—the main actions in the story. Sometimes they include what people said. After revision lessons with different types of details they can use, such as a character's thinking, a description of the setting, or "show, not tell," children as young as first grade can learn to go back and add these details in. Refer to CCSS Writing Standard 3 or the Units of Study books for grade-level-specific expectations (Calkins and colleagues 2013), but for first grade:

Narrative Writing Look-Fors: Elaboration

Question to Ask	Where to Look	The Ideal
Does the writer use any of the following types of detail: setting, character description or development, action, narration, internal thinking?	Sentence by sentence, notice the types of details the student uses to develop his piece.	A student should attempt to use different types of detail.
How well is each type of detail used?	Sentence by sentence, consider if the details make sense.	Details should help to move the story along and not confuse the reader.
Is the writer able to use temporal words to signal the passage of time?	Look at the beginning of each page (if the student is writing in a booklet) or in the beginning, middle, and end of the story if not.	The student uses some words to signal time is passing.

Conventions refers to the writer's ability to use grammar and punctuation in a way that aids in the meaning of the piece. The CCSS give very precise advice in the Language Standards strand about what conventions students should have control of by the end of each grade level. Keep in mind that when a child seems to have a certain convention under control, and then suddenly starts confusing it, it's possible the child is trying out something more complex. For example, many children in first grade can correctly construct and punctuate a simple subject and predicate sentence. But when they try to write compound sentences, or add adjectives, they may get confused about where the ending punctuation belongs. This new confusion should be seen as an exciting development as it offers a new opportunity for instruction.

For first graders, consider:

Narrative Writing Look-Fors: Conventions

Question to Ask	Where to Look	The Ideal
What does the student understand about spelling?	Take note of the types of words the student tends to spell incorrectly and those the child spells correctly. See if you can notice a pattern about the features of the words (e.g., vowel blends, multisyllabic words, words with inflected endings).	First graders, according to the CCSS, should be able to use conventional spelling for words with common spelling patterns and for frequently occurring irregular words. They should also be able to spell untaught words phonetically, drawing on phonemic awareness and spelling conventions.
What does the student understand about sentence structure?	Take note of the types and varieties of sentences the writer includes within the piece (e.g., fragments, run-ons, compound, complex, simple, and so on).	Children should use singular and plural nouns with matching verbs in basic sentences. They should also be able to use verbs to convey a sense of past, present, and future. Simple sentences and compound sentences should be grammatically correct.
What does the student understand about punctuation?	Look for how the child uses punctuation, both correctly and incorrectly.	The CCSS lists three end-of-year expectations for first graders. They should be able to capitalize dates and names of people, use end punctuation for sentences, and use commas in dates and to separate single words in a series.

A Sample Analysis: Marelle
Qualities of Good Writing

Marelle's booklet contains two different stories (Figure 2.21). The first story is about playing volleyball with her friend Aylin. The second story is about the time a dog came in her house. Both stories are very short and are focused on one main action.

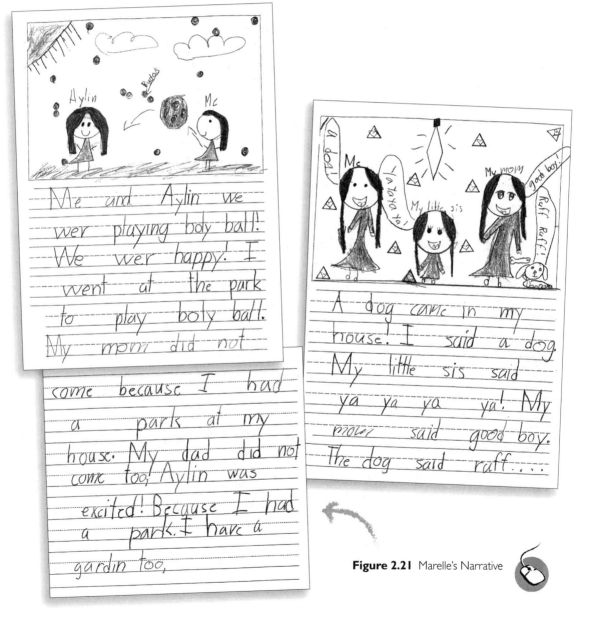

Me and Aylin we wer playing boly ball! We wer happy. I went at the park to play boly ball. My mom did not come because I had a parks at my house. My dad did not come too, Aylin was excited! Because I had a park. I have a gardin too.

A dog came in my house! I said a dog. My little sis said ya ya ya ya! My mom said good boy. The dog said raff....

Figure 2.21 Marelle's Narrative

In terms of structure, her stories begin with the main action she intends to use to focus the story (i.e., "Me and Aylin we were playing boly ball!" [sic]). Neither story has a sense of closure or an ending. She could use more support with understanding a beginning–middle–end story structure.

One way Marelle elaborates is by naming, but not describing, the setting (i.e., "the park" and "my house"). There is more setting description in her pictures than in her words. She states character feelings ("We were happy!") frequently in one story and what characters say ("My mom said good boy.") in the other. She does not yet use more than one type of detail in a single story. It's possible that she is trying to use whatever type of detail her teacher teaches on that day but isn't yet able to integrate multiple types of detail. More detailed action to show the steps of what's happening, as opposed to just summarizing what happens in the story, would also be helpful to teach her.

She spells high-frequency sight words correctly, and the spelling mistakes she does make show that she is listening to the sounds she hears and is using her knowledge of phonics to record appropriate letters for those sounds (i.e., *gardin* instead of *garden*). She punctuates her sentences correctly most of the time. She does not yet use quotation marks when writing dialogue, though this is not a grade-level expectation.

How I'd Summarize My Findings

Tool	Strengths	Possibilities for Growth
Narrative	• Writes separate events on separate pages	• Recognize story structure—beginning, middle, end
	• Something happens in the story	• Understand how events in the story connect to the main "happening" of the story
	• Uses character names, feelings, actions, dialogue, in separate stories	
		• Write with detailed action
	• Spells known words correctly	
		• Incorporate more than one type of detail within each story
	• Uses logical spelling for unknown words	

Excerpt from main table on pages 97–99

☐ Studying Writing Engagement

In addition to the qualities of good writing of an on-demand or published piece of writing, it's also important to consider a child's writing *process*. If you have a child's entire writing folder for a period of time, you'll also be able to get a sense of the child's total volume of writing, which will give you insight as well into her *engagement* and *stamina* when it comes to writing. For a first grader, consider:

What to Look For

Process, Engagement, and Stamina Look-Fors

Question to Ask	Where to Look	The Ideal
How would you describe the student's volume of writing?	Notice how much a child produces—in pictures and in words—in a given day. Notice if volume increases across the year.	A first grader writing in five-page booklets with a space for pictures and five or more lines on each page should be able to complete a booklet in a couple of days. In a week, the child should be able to write two to three complete stories.
Does the student have a process?	Observe what happens from the time the child selects new, blank paper on which to write.	Ideally, there is evidence of planning, drafting, and revising/editing. At this age, a child will typically plan a story by telling the story, touching each page as she goes. She will then sketch pictures quickly to "hold onto" what she wants to say on each page of a booklet. She'll then go back to page 1, writing the words that go with each picture. After the entire draft is down, she will go back to reread to make changes, additions, deletions; to revise; and/or to edit.

A Sample Analysis: Marelle

Marelle plans her writing before beginning to draft. During the thirty- to forty-minute observation, Marelle decided to choose blank paper and start a new piece. She planned out what she wanted to write on one page by telling her story to herself while touching the page. She then began drawing a picture at the top of that same page. Her drawing was *very* detailed, so much so that she spent almost the entire workshop period on illustrations and only got a few sentences of writing down (Figure 2.22).

For her to practice getting more words on the page, it would be important to teach Marelle to return to some of the stories she's planned out from earlier writing workshop sessions (there were several in her folder with illustrations only). It would also help if Marelle drew quicker sketches, just enough to hold the thought, and went back during revision to add more to her pictures and words. Planning across pages—what she intended to write in the beginning, middle, and end—might also help with her structure.

From the other work in her writing folder, it seems that Marelle is usually focused on drafting new pieces, rather than going back to improve (through revision and/or editing) the pieces she has already written.

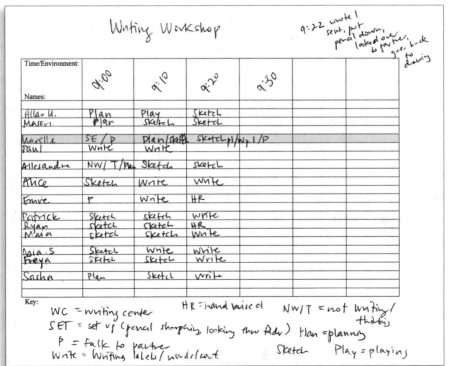

Figure 2.22 Writing Workshop Engagement Inventory

How I'd Summarize My Findings

Here's a summary of my takeaways about Marelle's engagement during writing and her writing process:

Tool	Strengths	Possibilities for Growth
Engagement inventory—writing workshop	• Uses a plan, sketch, write process • Draws before writing • Plans one part of the story by sketching, and then writes on that page • Draws detailed sketches	• Set up for writing more quickly • Make sketches more quickly to get to writing (volume) • Plan out the entire story (beginning, middle, end) before beginning to write • Spend less time sketching, more writing

Excerpt from main table on pages 97–99

☐ Making Discoveries from Informational Writing

Informational writing is an umbrella term that incorporates a variety of types of structures and subgenres, including all-about books, question-and-answer books, field guides, and reference materials. Informational writing tries to teach the reader, or inform the reader, about a topic. This writing may be research-based or based on personal expertise, though in the primary elementary grades it's usually the latter.

Several elements differentiate informational writing from narrative writing. Informational pieces are focused by a topic as opposed to an event or sequence of events in time. Instead of a sequence of events, informational writing will be organized into sections or parts. Instead of elaborating with dialogue and setting, informational writing will elaborate with factual information and added explanation on those facts.

For a list of grade-level expectations for informational writing, see the CCSS Writing Standard 2.

What to Look For

Remember that as we approach an example of student writing, we are going to look at it through different lenses. These lenses, or the *qualities of good writing*, will help us to see more and say more about the artifact. Here, again, are the categories:

- focus
- structure
- elaboration
- conventions

Let's look at each category to see how it can help us frame our analysis of a student's informational writing.

Focus refers to the extent to which the piece is focused on a broad or narrow topic. For example, one student might write about animals, and another might write about pets, and still another might write only about dogs. The more focused the writing, the more challenging it is to elaborate. You may also look to see how the writer is able to maintain the focus throughout the piece. For example, if a writer says she is writing about a Golden Retriever but then has a chapter called "all kinds of dogs," that child might be broadening her focus to add more detail. You can find grade-level specific expectations in the CCSS Writing Standard 2, or the Units of Study series (Calkins and colleagues 2013). The following table includes some general questions to consider and expectations to have when looking at a first grader's writing.

Informational Writing Look-Fors: Focus

Question to Ask	Where to Look	The Ideal
Is the focus established early in the piece?	The sentence (or page, if writing in a booklet) of the piece	The writer establishes the focus by stating the topic.
Does the conclusion for the piece match the initial focus?	The final page or sentence of the piece	The last sentence or page should give some sense of closure (i.e., "So now you know everything about dogs!").

continues

Informational Writing Look-Fors: Focus (cont.)

Question to Ask	Where to Look	The Ideal
How focused of a topic does the writer choose?	Consider how the topic could be made more general/broad or more specific/focused	It's unlikely that a child of this age will be able to manipulate the level of focus in his piece without a great deal of guidance. What's more important at this age and stage is that all of the pages/facts do relate to the topic the writer establishes early on in the piece.

To examine the *structure* in informational writing you might look at the overall structure and then at the structure of each part. First, you may ask yourself, "Does there appear to be an introduction of the topic, some elaboration with facts, and then a closure?" To look at the structure within a part, you may want to see if the facts within one part all relate. For example, if a child is writing about dogs and one of the pages is titled "Poodles," you can look to see if all of the facts on that page are about poodles. Reference CCSS Writing Standard 2, or the Units of Study series (Calkins and colleagues 2013) for grade-specific information. When you look at your first-grade student's writing, consider:

Informational Writing Look-Fors: Structure

Question to Ask	Where to Look	The Ideal
Is the piece organized into an introduction, body, and ending?	Scan to see if the child sets up/establishes the focus (on the first page or in the first sentence(s)), elaborates with some facts/details, and then closes (on a final page/final sentences).	The writer should establish the focus, elaborate on the focus, and then give a closing.
Is there structure within each part?	Look at one page of the student's writing.	The student should keep all related facts together.

Elaboration in an informational piece of writing should be factual. The writer may also include details that elaborate upon those facts. Facts may be from personal expertise or from information learned from other sources—by talking to peers or adults with information on the topic, reading a book about the topic, and/or watching a video about the topic, for example. Writers may elaborate on those facts by including more explanation, a definition of a term, or a response to the fact.

One other consideration is the vocabulary that a child uses when writing about a topic. For example, when writing about dogs, a writer should use words like *bark* and *leash* not just *brown* and *walk*. For grade-level-specific expectations, see CCSS Writing Standard 2, or Calkins and colleagues' Units of Study series (2013). For a first grader, consider:

Informational Writing Look-Fors: Elaboration

Question to Ask	Where to Look	The Ideal
What types of information does the writer include?	Across the piece, look to see the types of information—both facts and details to elaborate on the facts.	The writer establishes the focus by stating the topic.
How concrete are the details the writer includes?	When the writer is writing about a topic or concept, notice whether the details feel vague or specific.	The facts should be specific (i.e., "Walk your dog on a leash" instead of just "Walk your dog").
How precise is the vocabulary the writer uses?	Notice whether the author uses content-specific vocabulary.	Vocabulary is appropriate to the topic.

In looking at the student piece with the lens of *conventions*, consider the same set of questions laid out in the "Narrative Writing" section.

A Sample Analysis: Marelle

Marelle doesn't have any recent informational writing to analyze.

You will find that children, especially those in the primary grades, develop very quickly, so a piece of writing from the last unit of study a month ago will provide you with an outdated picture. It is more important to look at work that is current, and if you're working in a writers' workshop within units of study, it's not going to be possible to gather writing that represents informational, opinion, and narrative writing from the same couple of weeks.

Making Discoveries from Opinion Writing

Opinion writing is also an umbrella term that includes many types of writing. Children in younger grades may first try their hand at opinion writing by crafting letters that try to persuade someone of something (such as a letter to the school principal to change the lunch menu) or a review of something (the student's favorite video game). In later elementary school, writers may write thesis-driven types of writing such as essays or speeches.

Although the structures of these different types of writing may vary slightly, what they all have in common is that the author has a clear viewpoint, or opinion, and is setting about trying to convince the reading audience of that opinion. Often, the writer will support his opinion with reasons and information in an attempt to persuade his audience.

The CCSS Writing Standard 1 relates to opinion writing; refer to that document for grade-specific expectations. You can also consult the Units of Study series (Calkins and colleagues 2013).

What to Look For

As with the other two main categories of writing (narrative and informational), the qualities of good writing are helpful to use when examining opinion writing. Again, those categories are:

- focus
- structure
- elaboration
- conventions

When a writer attempts to *focus* an opinion piece of writing, the writing will be focused on that writer's opinion. The age and sophistication of the writer will depend on the sophistication of the idea. In first grade, "I want" or "I like" are very accessible ways to frame a claim. When looking at an opinion piece of writing, consider CCSS Writing Standard 1. This a summary of what you might look for in a first grader's opinion piece:

Opinion Writing Look-Fors: Focus

Question to Ask	Where to Look	The Ideal
Is the writer's opinion clear?	Read the first sentence and/or page.	Typically, a writer will state the claim or opinion up front, at the beginning of the piece.
Does the writer maintain support for his opinion throughout the piece?	Read the rest of the piece to see if there are reasons to support the opinion.	The writer should support the claim with at least one reason for the opinion.

The *structure* of an opinion piece may, at first blush, look something like an informational piece. Ideally, for a first grader, the piece begins with an introduction where the writer states the opinion, follows with a reason for that opinion, and concludes with a final closing sentence. The structure may vary somewhat by type of opinion writing. For example, a book review is slightly different in organization than a letter. You can ask yourself the same questions about structure for informational and opinion writing. See CCSS Writing Standard 1, and Calkins and colleagues' (2013) Units of Study series for more grade-specific expectations.

For first-grade writers, consider the following as you read the piece:

Opinion Writing Look-Fors: Structure

Question to Ask	Where to Look	The Ideal
Does the piece have a logical organization?	Look to see the order in which the following are included in the piece: the opinion, the reasons, the examples, the closing.	The writer should begin the piece with the opinion (in an opening, or introduction), elaborate with at least one reason, and provide some closure.

The *elaboration* of an opinion piece will likely include at least one reason, maybe more, and perhaps an example. For example, if the writer is trying to persuade the audience that "Dogs make the best pet," then one reason might be "You can play with them." An example that would support the reason could be "You can play fetch." As you look at your students' writing, consider CCSS Writing Standard 1, Calkins and colleagues' (2013) Units of Study series and/or the following guiding questions. Keep in mind the chart includes expectations for a first grader:

Opinion Writing Look-Fors: Elaboration

Question to Ask	Where to Look	The Ideal
Does the reason match the opinion?	After the writer states the opinion, look to see what sentences follow to explain why she thinks that.	The reason(s) should logically match the opinion.
Does the child elaborate with examples?	After a reason is stated, look to see if there is an example.	At this age, students aren't expected to always have examples, but if they do, the example(s) should match the reason(s).

Refer again to the previous section, "Narrative Writing," and the CCSS Language Standards as you consider the strength of the student's control of *conventions*.

A Sample Analysis: Marelle

Marelle does not have any opinion writing in her writing folder at this point in the year, as her class is working within a narrative unit of study. As I mentioned in the previous section on informational writing, it's more important to be looking at work from a finite period of time than it is to be looking at samples from every genre. If you work in units of study, each lasting several weeks, it's likely that you'll only be looking at one type of writing during this sample analysis.

ACTION ⟶

Now's the time to take a look at your student's writing or Emre's narrative. Remember that you can see my thinking about Emre's work in Appendix A, which you can use to compare against your own interpretations.

☐ Wrap-Up

Phew. You made it. If you've made your way through this chapter, learning about reading and writing artifact by artifact, working to understand Marelle as well as another student, you've probably spent a good deal of time. You might be wondering, "How in the world am I going to do this with all thirty of my students?" I'd say that you don't necessarily have to. This process might be most helpful for your Response to Intervention–identified students who might benefit from a close and careful look at their work, which could help you to craft a more meaningful goal. Or perhaps you'll take the time with a student you're trying to challenge, but seems to have it all down. Or maybe you try to do this once each year with each student, but at different times across the year. I have a few pieces of good news for you.

First, it'll get easier. Not right away, but the more you go through this process you'll find that things just jump off the page at you where before you had to study and study to figure out a student's strengths and needs.

Second, you hopefully learned a lot of content by working through this process so far. You learned what questions to ask of the data, and what it looks like when a student's work shows strong understanding. Hopefully you also identified gaps in your *own* content knowledge. For example, maybe you've realized that for years you've only had your students write narratives and you want to study up on how qualities of good writing apply to informational writing. You may look back at Chapter 1 for some suggested professional reading to help with whatever goal you have articulated for yourself.

Third, this work is going to pay off big time. By looking this closely at your student's work you're going to be choosing teaching that will make a big difference and will help you to see dramatic progress.

ACTION ⟶ *Jot Down Your Ideas*

Reflect to set professional goal(s) for yourself. Think about which piece(s) of student work you found it most difficult to analyze. What are the areas of reading (engagement, fluency, print work, comprehension, conversation) or writing (qualities of good writing in narrative, opinion, or informational texts or writing engagement, process, or stamina) that those examples of student work align with? Check back in Chapter 1 where I make professional reading recommendations and consider getting a professional text on order!

Write notes here:

_____

_____

_____

_____

What's Next?

In the next chapter, I'm going to walk you through the next step of the process: synthesizing the data and setting a goal. It's here that we'll take what we noticed about each individual piece of data, put it together, and notice patterns and trends. Make sure you have your one complete table with strengths and needs ready to go.

Chapter 3

Interpreting Data and Establishing a Goal

> Set goals—high goals . . .
> When [you have] a goal
> to shoot for, you create
> teamwork, people working
> for a common good.
> —**Paul William
> "Bear" Bryant**

I was with some kindergarteners on a field trip to the zoo when Desiree tugged on my shirt just inches from the giraffe enclosure, pointed obviously (and embarrassingly) at another zoo-goer, and stage whispered, "Ms. Serravallo, that's a *girl,* right?" The person she was pointing to had long hair in a ponytail, was wearing construction boots—and also had a beard.

Teachable moment, I thought to myself. This is a chance to tell Desiree that she can be anything she wants to be, dress and express herself any way she chooses, and pick a career that matters most to her—just as the man at the zoo had chosen to wear his hair long! But maybe she didn't need the elaborate *celebrate our differences* lecture I wanted to give. She was simply collecting data and trying to make an interpretation based on the facts before her. She wasn't being judgmental—she literally just wanted to know if the person was male or female. But when she looked across the information she was gathering, she wasn't sure what conclusion to draw. From her prior knowledge, beard meant male and long hair meant female.

There is something about humans that makes us want to instantly put people (and things) in boxes, assign labels, and create clear distinctions. It feels comforting; not knowing can create a sense of cognitive dissonance.

For us teachers, the same may be true. We may meet a student and think, "He's just like ____ from last year's class" or "I've seen that before. This is the kid who needs ____." After all, the process we take to turn the data in front of us into goals and instruction is interpretation. And interpretation comes from leaning on our own mind-sets, experiences, and prior knowledge and applying it to our students. Just as Desiree jumped to an interpretation that the man was female based on his ponytail, we might jump to a conclusion about a student based on something we find to be a particularly salient and relevant detail about their reading and/or writing. For many of us, this might be a child's tendency to write with hard to read spelling. Or maybe it's a child's fidgetiness during independent work time.

In this chapter, I'll lead you through the process of making interpretations about the student work you analyzed during the previous chapter—student work that offers the kind of information you can use to make sound teaching decisions.

Upon arriving at this chapter, the most time-consuming part of this process is behind you: analyzing each piece of data separately to name what it says about a student's strengths and needs. If you have been following along using your own student's work (or the samples from Emre included in Appendix A), you now have a complete table listing out many possible avenues for instruction. Here's where we are in the process:

- Step 1: Collect data.
- Step 2: Analyze data.
- **Step 3: Interpret data and establish a goal.**
- Step 4: Create an action plan.

Marvel at all you've discovered about Emre, or the student whose work you've chosen to study. Some of it you may have already known. Some of it may be new. Some of it may even contradict what you *thought* you knew.

This discovery contradicting prior knowledge used to happen all the time when I was a teacher, and it happens all of the time when I lead teachers through this protocol. A teacher will bring a stack of work and begin with a disclaimer or preface about the student. Recently, a second-grade teacher brought the work of a child she was concerned about because the child seemed stuck in superficial-level comprehension and thinking when he reads and writes. His narratives lacked insight and his reading work was mostly retelling. By going through this process, however, we discovered that the biggest thing we could do to help him was actually to teach him strategies for staying focused and engaged in his work—once we went down that path, he became much more interpretive!

What's fascinating to me about the process of following the four-step protocol described in this book is that it will often illuminate one of our own habitual missteps in trying to teach in a data-based way. Sometimes, it's our tendency as teachers to focus heavily on the most salient observations, falsely assuming that because it's the most obvious, it's also the most important. Or perhaps it's that you'll realize that the work you've been collecting and using to form goals all along really didn't provide the depth you thought it did. Or perhaps you found that you were sometimes making excuses for students, explaining away their lack of progress with something that really is unrelated to the work they are doing in the classroom.

Missteps aside, this chapter will help you take all the information, all the possibilities you've arrived at thus far through analysis of the data, and make a decision about what to teach. We'll be sorting through all the possible areas for growth to arrive at a clear goal—one that spans both reading and writing. One that will focus the differentiated instruction for weeks or maybe even months to come. One that will make the biggest difference for each student in your class.

○ Why Is Goal Setting Important?

Think for a moment about the last time you were proud of an accomplishment. When you set out to accomplish what you did, do you remember stating a goal at the outset? "I want to run that marathon," or "This year I'm going to commit to eating out less and cooking at home more," or "This weekend we're going to organize that garage so I can fit my car inside." Goals affect accomplishment—when we have a clear sense of what we want to accomplish, how we will attempt to accomplish it, and our deadline for accomplishing it, we are more likely to be motivated to succeed (Pink 2011).

Reading and writing are no different. Stated goals hold students and their teachers accountable. When goals come from an accurate assessment of what's really going on with a reader, when they are decided upon in conversation with the student and supported over time, readers will accomplish more and succeed more.

Hattie (1999) and Petty (2006) have shown in their research that "achievement is enhanced to the degree that students and teachers set and communicate appropriate, specific, and challenging goals" (Petty, 63). Fisher, Frey, and Lapp (2012) agree: "Goal setting should be a regular part of the instructional design process" (81). You are now ready to begin setting that appropriate, specific, and challenging goal with your student, and to begin helping the student toward increased achievement. Ideally, you'll decide on a goal using the data you've collected, and then, in conversation with the student and through careful questioning, you'll help her to recognize and understand what you've discovered.

Once a goal is established, you'll teach and provide feedback to the student over time about his progress toward that goal. Feedback is shown to have a major influence on performance (Hattie 1999). Ericsson, Krampe, and Tesch-Römer (1993) note that motivation does not always come from enjoyment of the task alone (although of course we want children to enjoy reading and writing!) but rather from recognizing that hours of practice will yield increased performance. They advocate "repeated experiences in which the individual can attend to the critical aspects of the situation and incrementally improve her or his performance in response to knowledge of results, feedback, or both from a teacher" (398).

So, of the long list you've created of possible areas for growth, which one do you pick? To help my decision making, I tend to do two things: I look for patterns, and then I apply the 80/20 principle, which I'll explain in detail in the section that follows.

Looking for Patterns: Triangulating the Data

To choose a goal that is going to have the biggest possible effect on a student's progress, it's got to be something important. The goal needs to be something for which you see instructional opportunity in both reading and writing, so that when you and the student are working on the goal, you have opportunities across the day to practice. Seeing the same teaching opportunity when looking at more than one work artifact also tells you that the need wasn't a fluke—it wasn't a result of the assignment or task, and it wasn't a result of the student missing breakfast one day or being distracted by an argument with his mom that morning.

When I look at the long list of options, I often try to triangulate—or at least *bi*angulate—the data. I try to see where a potential area of growth crops up in more than one place, examining more than one artifact, in both reading and writing. Sometimes, in working toward this kind of synthesis, I may realize that I didn't state a similar goal in the exact same way in each artifact, but if I can adjust and restate, more than one possible goal will fit together.

Let's look together at the table we've created by studying Marelle's work (Figure 3.1).

Tool	Strengths	Possibilities for Growth
Engagement inventory—reading workshop	• Has strategies to set herself up for a successful reading period • Can sustain reading for long periods of time • Smiles in response to her reading	• Shorten setup time to maximize independent reading
Reading interest inventory	• Finds a place to read that works for her • Knows what kinds of books she enjoys	• Expand her definition of reading as more than about reading the "hard words" • Support her in making meaning and understanding the story
Writing about reading	• Rephrases what happens in the story • Has a simple idea about a character ("funny")	• Infer further beyond the story

Figure 3.1 Table Created from Studying and Analyzing Marelle's Work   *continues*

Tool	Strengths	Possibilities for Growth
Fluency (from fluency record)	• 2- to 3-word phrases consistently, some 4-word phrases • Reads dialogue with expression	• 3- to 4-word phrases consistently, using the natural phrasing (sentence broken across lines) to support her
Running record	• Uses visual and syntactical cueing systems consistently • Occasionally uses meaning • Retell captures most important information from beginning, middle, end • Reads sight words automatically • Self-corrects using visual information	• Use meaning consistently • Errors that sounded right but didn't make sense were probably due to lack of vocabulary/background knowledge • Work to self-correct using meaning and/or syntax
Partnership—reading workshop	• Retells details from her book • Rereads a familiar book with confidence • Sticks to one topic of conversation • Answers questions comfortably	• Give ideas, not just retell • Offer questions to her partner • Choose a part to reread for a purpose
Narrative	• Writes separate events on separate pages • Something happens in the story	• Recognize story structure—beginning, middle, end • Understand how events in the story connect to the main "happening" of the story

continues

Tool	Strengths	Possibilities for Growth
Narrative, cont.	• Uses character names, feelings, actions, dialogue, in separate stories • Spells known words correctly • Uses logical spelling for unknown words	• Write with detailed action • Incorporate more than one type of detail within each story
Engagement inventory—writing workshop	• Uses a plan, sketch, write process • Draws before writing • Plans one part of the story by sketching, and then writes on that page • Draws detailed sketches	• Set up for writing more quickly • Make sketches more quickly to get to writing (volume) • Plan out the entire story (beginning, middle, end) before beginning to write • Spend less time sketching, more writing

As I look at this chart during this phase of the protocol, I'm going to focus on the third column, "Possibilities for Growth." I can focus my attention only on that column because I am confident that when doing my initial analysis, I made sure that every possible area of growth comes from a strength. I'm aiming to state a possible goal and to back up my decision with evidence from my analysis of Marelle's work with more than one data tool. I use a language frame—a sort of template—to force me to seek out patterns as I craft a goal for Marelle, so that an idea of lesser importance doesn't just jump off the page and demand my attention:

I think [student] could learn [possible goal in reading] and [related possible goal in writing] because in reading, I noticed [findings from column #3] and in writing I noticed [findings from column #3].

In this step of the protocol, I also try to be sure to push myself to name *several* possible goals. My thinking about this is similar to my thinking about the need to triangulate. I want to make sure that I'm not just grasping at any isolated idea that jumps off the page.

In doing this work with hundreds of teachers, I've found that it's often the case that the first thing you see as a teacher is the thing you *want* to see—the thing you expect to see. Or sometimes, it's the thing that is *your thing* as a teacher. Some of us tend to fixate on grammar, others are big on the importance of details and description, others care most about deep interpretive reading. By listing out several possibilities, you're forcing yourself to think beyond your first gut instinct, and you may end up landing on an option that is more important for a student. I try to articulate four or five goals at this stage.

For Marelle, here are five possible goals and the evidence for why I think these goals might matter for her:

> *Possible goal #1: I think Marelle could focus more on using meaning in reading and on elaboration in writing. In reading, when asked questions about her reading, she talks about how reading to her is about reading hard words. Also, she tends to use visual cueing systems most consistently, and meaning inconsistently. In writing, she tends to leave pieces unfinished, not elaborating past the initial focus of the piece.*
>
> *Possible goal #2: I think Marelle could focus more on having ideas about her books in reading and on elaboration in writing. When she talks or writes about her reading, she tends to recall actions in the story without saying more and giving her own ideas. In writing, her elaboration tends to be sparse and only one type (i.e., dialogue or feeling but not both) per piece.*

ACTION →

Take out the summary table of your ideas about Emre. Try this same work of naming several possible goals and backing up your thinking by providing evidence across pieces of data. When possible, look across reading and writing. Jot your thoughts down first, and then take a look in Appendix A to see my thinking.

Possible goal #3: I think Marelle could use support with structure/organization in writing and with retelling/sequencing in reading. In writing, Marelle tends to plan and write just one page and leave the middle and end unfinished, and consequently many pieces are without a clear beginning–middle– end structure. In reading, she can retell in sequence (as on her running record) when she is flipping through the pages, but when talking about her book with a partner or when writing about her reading, she tends to focus on just one part of the book.

Possible goal #4: I think Marelle could practice expressive language more in both reading and writing. During partnership time in both reading and writing, she will answer questions given to her briefly but doesn't initiate conversation or ask questions of her partners.

Possible goal #5: I think Marelle could work on her fluency in both reading and writing. In reading, she could work to read in longer phrases. In writing, she could work to plan what she wants to say and then get the writing down faster on her page.

To finalize the goal-setting process, I will either choose one of them to begin working on with Marelle or decide to further synthesize, putting a couple of related goals together. When choosing a goal, I use the 80/20 principle.

Applying the 80/20 Principle: Choosing a Goal

The 80/20 principle, also known as the "Pareto principle" or the "Pareto rule," refers to the idea that 20 percent of something has the potential to cause or create 80 percent result. To put it another way, a minority of input can yield a majority of output. Pareto first made this observation in Italy in relation to economics. Pareto noticed that 80 percent of Italy's land was owned by 20 percent of the population. He then carried out surveys on a variety of other countries and found to his surprise that a similar distribution applied (Koch 2008; Gladwell 2002).

This statistical finding has implications for your personal life (20 percent of what you do accounts for 80 percent of your happiness), for business (80 percent of revenue comes from 20 percent of initiatives), and even in the teaching of reading and writing. In reading and writing, I'd like to assert that one goal of the five I articulated will make 80 percent of the difference in Marelle's reading and writing life.

In essence, I try to work smarter, not harder. I try to find the 20 percent thing that makes the 80 percent difference. I try to focus my energies and efforts, and I help the student to do so as well.

Looking across all of the possibilities for what would help the student, what one thing will make the biggest difference? What 20 percent of her reading and writing needs, when worked on consistently over the next month or so, will yield an 80 percent improvement? What are the goals that might impact other goals? For example, focusing on improving Marelle's expressive language (#4) could help her to say more about her reading and write more in her stories (#2). Helping Marelle organize her writing better and understand story structure better in reading (#3) could also help her to elaborate, as she'll now have entire parts to her stories to talk about (#2). Understanding structure better in reading and writing may also help with meaning (#1) because she'll understand how all the parts of a story fit together. Teaching her the importance of meaning (#1) could help with her fluency (#5) as well as improve her reading level.

I want to choose a goal that I think has the potential to impact the others. To me, structure needs to come first. If you teach a student to add in more detail without the structure, the detail can start to become overwhelming and confusing. Without a sense of story structure when reading or retelling what you've read, the details don't logically connect. I want Marelle to understand what she's reading, think that meaning is an important reason to read, and to consider what she wants to say when she writes. To me, the first step at doing all of this is goal #3 (in the hopes that it also has a major ripple effect into goal #1).

ACTION →

Apply the 80/20 principle to Emre's goals, or the goals of the student you're investigating. Articulate your final decision about the student's goal. To see my thinking about Emre's work, turn to Appendix A.

The First Teaching Opportunity: The Goal-Setting Conference

Now that you have articulated a goal for your student, it's time to sit the student down for a goal-setting conference. In my mind, the goal-setting conference is the first conference occurring after the teacher has chosen a goal to work toward. After this conference, with the support of the next chapter, you will plan strategies and methods for ongoing instruction—but first, it's important to get the student on board.

It's well established that the more a person takes ownership of her own goal, the more likely it is that the goal will be accomplished (see, for example, Pink 2011). The more we can lead students toward the articulation of their own goals, the more investment they will have in working to accomplish that goal.

I say "lead students" because without your leadership, it's likely that the student would choose a more superficial, obvious, or basic goal. Ask a student to articulate a goal without any guidance, and the student will usually say something like, "I want to read harder books," or "I want to read faster," or "I'm going to try to write longer stories." This "longer, faster, more" is generally what students believe makes for a better reader or writer.

On the other hand, participating in a goal-setting conference that is grounded in some of the student's own data, with a conversation guided by your careful questioning, can help a student to realize things about her work or process or skill level that she may not have otherwise considered.

Now, you haven't spent all of this time analyzing the student's work for the student to choose some goal from out in left field. You'll need to be prepared to steer the conversation toward helping the student realize for himself what you've realized in his absence. So it will take some degree of skill on your part to help lead the child to notice what you noticed.

Be sure to gather only the work from your stack that would help a child to notice what you noticed. For example, if you want the student to notice her tendency toward being distracted, you might choose to have the child's reading log (which would show very little being read during each sitting) and writing folder (which would show just one or two unfinished pieces).

For Marelle, I would present her writing and compare it to writing from other students in the class who have a clear beginning, middle, and end. Any time you ask students to do reflection where they compare their work against that of another student's, it's important to be mindful of the language you use in how you present it so as not to set up a feeling of inferiority in any student. Saying things like, "Let's get some ideas for what other things you can do" has a different tone than "Let's look to see what you're not doing yet from this other student's piece so you can be a better writer, like her."

I would also show her some of her writing about reading and ask her to talk about how much of the book she's thinking about when she writes. See Figure 3.2 for more ideas of what you might plan to gather based on what your goal is.

Gathering Materials for the Goal-Setting Conference

Sample Goal	Materials to Use During the Goal-Setting Conference
Work on character inference when reading fiction, and on show, not tell when writing narratives	Sticky notes that show literal responses to reading, an action-only narrative without much description
Work on consistently using phonics rules for spelling (encoding) and reading (decoding)	Word work, writing, and/or a running record that shows certain spelling features are sometimes used and other times aren't
Work on focus and attention during reading and writing workshops	Reading logs that show a slow page-per-minute rate, or a lower-than-expected volume, and/or a writing folder with unfinished pieces or low volume

Figure 3.2

Once you've gathered the materials that will help the student realize the same potential area of growth that you did, you'll want to set aside about five to ten minutes to have a conversation with the student. I usually begin by stating my intention for our time together: that we're going to look over some of the student's work together and decide what one ambitious goal will make the biggest difference in his reading and writing for the next month or two. I state the intention in that way so that the goal setting becomes bigger than "I want to read every night for thirty minutes." Through my questioning and guidance, the goal will not only be ambitious but also specific.

Next, I lay the work on the table in front of us and ask the student to look with me. I'll ask the student what he notices about the work. This inquiry can often benefit from careful, leading questions (see page 105).

A side note about leading young children through inquiry: we teachers sometimes assume that it's important to tread very carefully with little kids, treat them gently, not cause any undue stress. Sometimes, though, we can mistake well-intentioned kindness for a lack of clarity in teaching. Many children—even the youngest ones—*like* seeing the specifics of what can be done better. Many find it satisfying to have clear goals and know what's expected in the classroom. By asking specific, clear questions and leading students to inquire about their own work and processes, it helps them to develop into thoughtful and reflective readers and writers.

Keep in mind that in most cases, if the student knew what she needed to do, she would just do it. The goal, although an outgrowth of a strength, is not yet something that is within the child's repertoire. Contrastive examples—another student's work, a rubric, or a sample of work from a prior lesson—could be helpful to lead the student through the inquiry.

After a few minutes of conversation with the student where you question and prompt her thinking, you'll want to establish a clear goal together. Chances are good that the student will need you to articulate the goal clearly. You might say something like, "So it sounds like a good goal for you would be to ____ in reading and ____ in writing."

As soon as the goal is clear, many find it helpful for the teacher or student to jot that goal on a sticky note, goal card, bookmark, or some other form to make it official. This tangible reminder of the goal will also be a way for the student, or her parents, and any other service providers to stay focused and clear on the work ahead. For young children, these personalized tools may not be just words on a sticky note stating a strategy, but may instead be a visual cue to remind them of what to do. For example, if you've just taught a child to always check to make sure what she's reading makes

Some Questions and Prompts to Use During Goal-Setting Conferences

- What can you notice about your work?
- How does your work compare to *(provide work of another student, an author, or exemplar)*?
- Can you think of any ways that you might improve your work?
- Let's talk about some of the things you think you're good at as a reader or writer.
- What do you think might be a good goal for you based on what we've noticed?
- When you look at your work, what are some things you seem to struggle with?
- Is there anything you notice from this (rubric, other student's work, etc.) that you think you'd like to try to start doing?
- What's going to make the biggest difference for you as a reader/writer?
- What is some new work you think you're ready to start taking on?
- One thing I notice is ____. What are your thoughts about that?

sense, looks right, and sounds right, you might draw an eye, a thought bubble, and an ear on a sticky note. For more information about using visuals as tools to support student independence, see Martinelli and Mraz's *Smarter Charts K–2* (2012).

Next, you'll help the student begin her journey toward accomplishing the goal with one clear strategy for either reading or writing that she can start right away. Make it clear that this is the first of many strategies you'll introduce during the upcoming weeks.

As with any opportunity for guided practice, it's helpful to not only mention the strategy but also to give the student a quick chance to try the work in front of you as you offer support. Don't fret if the student has yet to achieve perfection with the strategy—if she did, you might worry that your goal wasn't ambitious enough! Instead, make notes to yourself about the level of support the student needed as you practiced the strategy together.

End the conference by repeating the goal and the first strategy you offered to the student to begin work on the goal. Let the student know when you'll next see her and what you expect to happen between now and then. For example, are you expecting the student to write anything down to show she's been practicing what you just taught? Do you want the student to be ready to show you anything a few days from now? Based on how this student learns, you may choose to write this plan down as well.

Read the goal-setting conference that follows. I've included conferring tips embedded within the transcript to help elucidate some of the moves within the conference that are applicable to any conference. More about the structure of conferences can be found in the next chapter. As you read this conference, notice that I'm employing an inquiry approach. Notice my questioning techniques to try to support Marelle in noticing what I've noticed about her work.

Goal-Setting Conference with Marelle

T: Hi, Marelle. I've been spending some time looking at some of your work and I thought we could meet to talk about how your reading and writing has been going. We're going to look together and pick something for you to work on to get even stronger at reading and writing. I brought a few things for us to look at. I have some of your writing, and I have some of your writing about reading. I also brought Alessandra's story to take a look at so we can see what some other kids in the class are doing in case it will give us some ideas.

[I spread the work out on the table in front of us.]

M: *[nods]*

T: OK, so what we want to do here is to look at these three pieces of work and see if together we can find something you're strong at, but that you want to get even better at. Take a minute to look it over and tell me what you're thinking.

[Starting with strengths helps keep the tone of the conference positive and encouraging.]

M: I think I like to write stories and read stories.

T: I agree. This writing is a story of something that happened to you. And this sticky note has some of your thinking about what happened in a book. How does your work look compared to Alessandra's?

M: Well, she writes a lot more.

T: She does write more. Let's look closely and see how she does that. *[I read Alessandra's story, which is written across three pages with a clear beginning, middle, and end.]*

[Notice how I'm trying to leave the questioning open-ended, inviting inquiry. I want to support the student's noticing of her own work. When she says something seemingly simple or basic, I try to make a bigger deal of it, explicitly naming and elaborating on her strengths.]

M: She tells a whole long story.

T: When you say *long*, that makes me think that her story has different parts to it. Different things happen. Let's look at your story. How many things happen in your story?

[*This next part of the conference will take a bit more guidance. If Marelle already knew what she had to do to grow, she might just well do it! Providing ideas or examples of other students' work will help give the child an image of what to strive for.*]

M: I think just one thing in this story about the dog coming. The dog comes. And in this story, just one thing. I play volleyball.

T: That's great that you realized those are two different stories because different things happen. You know, when these were in your folder, these two pages were stapled together as if they were one story. So, do you think that's something you'd want to try to learn about? How to stretch out your story so it's one big long story, across a few pages?

M: Yeah. I want to write a story with lots of pages.

T: OK, now let's see if we can think of a reading goal that goes with the writing goal.

M: I'm not sure.

T: Well, here I have something you wrote about your book [*reads sticky note*]. I brought the book you were reading when you wrote this. Let me ask you, how many pages of the book were you thinking about when you wrote this sticky note?

M: Well, I was thinking of this on this page so I wrote it here.

T: So you mean you wrote just about what happened on that page?

M: Yes.

T: Well, I wonder if I helped you think about the whole story—the beginning, the middle, and the end, just like we're going to think about writing a whole story—a beginning, a middle, and an end. Maybe you'd have more to say?

[I've now articulated the goal for her. The next step is to get her started with a strategy.]

M: And then I can write more and I can read more?

T: That's what I'm thinking. Let's start with writing. One thing that I notice is that sometimes you start with an idea of what you want to write, but then the story doesn't really end. When I plan my story, I like to plan on three pages. The three pages stand for the beginning, middle, and end of a story.

[Here I take out a prestapled booklet with three pages. There's a box at the top of each page for a picture, and lines below. The paper is the same as what she's been using, but the idea to have three pages representing a beginning, middle, and end is something she hasn't yet mastered.]

T: So we're going to tell a story—maybe even one of these that you started telling here. You're going to tell me how does it start [*I touch the first page*], what happens after that [*I touch the middle page*], and then how does the story end [*I touch the last page.*]

M: Well, first me and Aylin were playing volleyball.

T: OK, touch that first page. [*She does.*] Good. Now turn the page.

M: And then when we were playing we were happy.

T: OK, that's great detail because you told a character's feeling. But what *happened*?

M: We kept getting the ball over the net again and again and again.

T: OK, good, that's an action. That's something that happened. Now how does the story end?

M: Aylin went home.

T: Well that certainly ends it! Is there anything that happened right while you were still playing that would be like the end?

M: My mom said, "Girls, time to come in for dinner!"

T: I think that might be a better ending because it happened right there. See? You told me the beginning [*I touch the first page*], the middle [*I touch the second*], and the end [*I touch the last*]. If you write that story across all three pages, you'll have a story that makes sense and then we can go back and add more details later to make it even longer, like Alessandra's.

[*A large part of this conference is about leading the child through self-reflection. Although I do introduce a strategy, I don't spend an enormous amount of time working with her on it. This is the start of a goal that will focus her work in reading and writing for weeks to come. This is only the first meeting we'll have together. Most of the next conference will be spent with me supporting and guiding her work as she works using the strategy.*]

M: OK. Should I write it now?

T: Yes, why don't you draw a quick sketch on each page to remember what you're going to write, then go back and write it.

M: OK.

T: I'm going to leave you with this little chart that I made to remind you of the steps we just took. We said the story, touching each page. Next, you're going to sketch the pictures on each page, and last you're going to write [see Figure 3.3].

[*I'm leaving Marelle with a tangible artifact to support her as she practices independently. At this point, I finished up my notes before moving on to another student for a conference. This also establishes clear accountability—as if to say, "I spent this time with you, we set a goal, now I'm going to follow up with you and support you as you try it." I will stay for another minute to record some of my own notes (Figure 3.4).*]

Figure 3.3 Marelle's Personal Chart

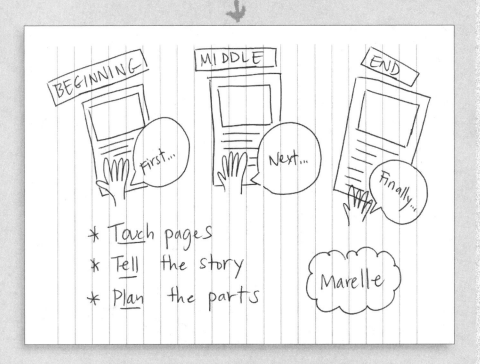

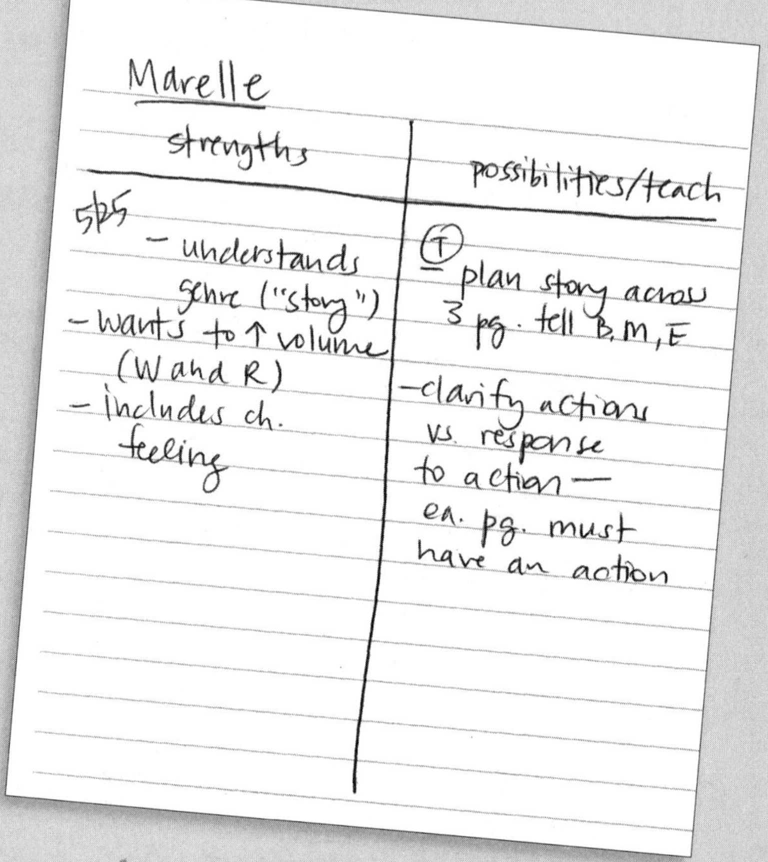

Marelle

strengths	possibilities/teach
SPS - understands genre ("story") - wants to ↑ volume (W and R) - includes ch. feeling	Ⓣ - plan story across 3 pg. tell B, M, E - clarify actions vs. response to action — ea. pg. must have an action

Figure 3.4 My Notes from the Conference

⬜ Wrap-Up

Synthesis is so challenging. Putting together many parts, seeing the overlap and the inconsistencies, and arriving at an interpretation: It is serious brain work. And, much like interpretations of your favorite book club book or last night's *Mad Men* episode, there isn't always one "right" answer.

What's most important in your interpretation of student data is that it's rooted in reality. Try as hard as possible not to let your preconceived notions of the student you're studying sway you away from what his work is telling you. By triangulating the data, you can be sure that the result isn't a fluke from the student having an off day. The result you see across situations shows that it's the most important thing to be working on for several weeks to come.

Before forging ahead, make sure you meet with the student in a goal-setting conference to ensure his buy-in. Having a student motivated and wanting to work on a goal will make progress and success happen much sooner than if you impose your thinking upon the student.

ACTION ⟶

If you're working with Emre's work samples, imagine the conference you'd have. What would you ask? What artifacts would you gather? Are there any contrastive examples (like the rubric I provided to Marelle) that would be helpful to have on hand during the conference? If you're working with a student from your own class, give this type of conferring a try.

⬜ What's Next?

In the next chapter, we're going to explore what it takes to turn a goal into an action plan. We'll look closely at the strategies and methods you'll craft and borrow. We'll consider how you might involve others (parents, intervention specialists) in the plan and how the plan will play out over time. Finally, we'll think about clarifying an image of what it will look like when the goal is accomplished.

Chapter 4

■■■■■■■■
■■■■■■■■

Creating an Action Plan

I'm putting the finishing touches on this book in late August, as the days are getting shorter, the weather is getting cooler, and teachers here in the Northeast are spending countless hours getting ready for the next crop of kids. Before all of the unpacking boxes, dusting, and hanging up bulletin boards, though, teachers no doubt spent some planning about how this year would be different.

Many of you probably spent time during the summer sketching out a map of how you'd arrange your furniture in your classroom. Some attended professional development workshops to hear the latest ideas on how to incorporate technology into the classroom and have decided to position the classroom meeting carpet under the SMART Board. Some of you may have gone to a conference where you heard new ideas about how to keep anecdotal records and are creating binders with divided, tabbed sections, one for each student. Still others of you might have thought about how to improve the home–school connection this year and have begun crafting letters home to parents, introducing yourselves and your dreams for the year to come.

I have always loved this August to September transition, for it is this time of year when all of the plans start to become action. To me, those who care to plan for the year ahead care enough to have hope and to make promises—to do something different, to try something new, to outgrow ourselves, to follow through.

In the past chapters, we've looked closely at student work, interpreted the patterns in the work, and decided on a goal. Now, it's time to make a plan and begin to turn that plan into action. Plans require a level of practicality, a level of *how to* to make them go from wishes and dreams to reality. And that's what we'll focus on in this chapter.

We have arrived at step 4:

- Step 1: Collect data.
- Step 2: Analyze data.
- Step 3: Interpret data and establish a goal.
- ## Step 4: Create an action plan.

To me, a solid action plan needs to be able to answer a few critical *how* questions:

1. *How will I plan for repeated practice* in terms of both *strategies* and *instructional formats*?
2. *How will the teaching look over time—who* will be involved (service providers, intervention specialists, parents) and *how* long will it take?
3. *How will I know* when the goal has been met?

It's usually at this point, when I'm explaining this protocol in a workshop, that those teachers who are familiar with SMART goals from the business and management world say that this is all sounding very familiar. SMART stands for:

- S—specific
- M—measurable
- A—attainable
- R—realistic
- T—timely

This is exactly what we're doing here. We've chosen a goal for a student that is specific and something she can attain, because it's rooted in current strengths. Now we need to make a plan that is realistic. Our plan needs to be time based and with a clear sense of what it will look like when it's been accomplished. In this way, we can begin to lead a student's work with clarity and focus.

Planning for Practice Over Time: Skills and Strategies

Once you've established a goal, there will no doubt be some skills the student will be working on for the goal to be accomplished. Skills may be things such as:

- reading with fluency
- inferring
- writing with more description
- decoding
- visualizing
- monitoring and self-correcting
- revising with purpose

A goal may relate to one skill or to multiple skills. To keep the work focused, it is important to declare and articulate the necessary skills. However, for students to be able to practice the work and eventually become skilled, I believe they need strategies for doing so.

As mentioned earlier, researchers, authors, and theorists may disagree about the use of the terms *skill* and *strategy* (see, for example, Keene and Zimmermann 2007; Afflerbach, Pearson, and Paris 2008; Serravallo 2010; Harvey and Goudvis 2007; Wiggins 2013), and it is for that reason that I am briefly defining what *I* mean so that you can follow my advice in this chapter.

> Strategies are deliberate and intentional actions a learner purposefully takes to accomplish a specific task or skill.

To me, strategies are deliberate and intentional actions a learner purposefully takes to accomplish a specific task or skill (Serravallo 2010). The strategy is step-by-step, a procedure or recipe. But the strategy is also a scaffold. Once the reader becomes skilled, the process becomes automatic and something the reader doesn't need to give conscious attention to. The need for the strategy fades away and likely only resurfaces in times of real difficulty.

Clarifying Goals, Skills, and Strategies

Goal—Large, Overarching, Will Take Weeks to Accomplish	Skills—Behaviors, Habits, Processes	Strategies—Procedural How-tos to Accomplish the Skill
Inferring about characters while reading, and adding more description to characters (in pictures and words) when writing	• Inferring • Determining importance • Adding detail when developing character	• Inferring: When reading, notice what a character says and does. Think about what kind of person would talk like or act like that. • Determining importance: Notice places where the character changes feelings in the story. That is often a moment where a major event has occurred. • Adding detail: When writing a story, think about describing the character with more detail. Think not only about what the character is doing, but also about what the character says and feels. Add more details to describe the character.
Monitoring for meaning and fixing up mistakes closer to the point of error	• Monitoring for meaning	• Monitoring for meaning: When writing, reread as you go. Track the words with your finger as you reread to ensure you aren't missing any words. • Monitoring for meaning: When reading, ask yourself, "Did that make sense, sound right, and look right?" If something doesn't, go back to fix it.

continues

Clarifying Goals, Skills, and Strategies (cont.)

Goal—Large, Overarching, Will Take Weeks to Accomplish	Skills—Behaviors, Habits, Processes	Strategies—Procedural How-tos to Accomplish the Skill
Working with more attention and focus during reading and writing workshops	• Choosing just-right books • Self-monitoring engagement • Refocusing • Visualizing • Building stamina	• Choosing just-right books: Look back across the last few weeks' worth of book logs. Notice the books you abandoned and those you stuck with. What are the patterns? Find books with similar traits as those you liked. • Building stamina: In longer books, set short-term goals for yourself. Place a sticky note or bookmark every certain number of pages (number will vary based on what the reader considers appropriate). When you get to the sticky note, check yourself. Did you understand what you read? Did you stay focused?
Developing concept of word/spacing	• One-to-one matching • Putting spaces between words	• One-to-one matching: Place a colored dot underneath single words in a level A/B text. Point to each dot while reading the word above it. • Spacing: Say what you want to write, count the words in your sentence. Draw a line on your writing for each word you hear with a space between each line. Go back and write the words on the lines. • Spacing: Say the word, write the word, put two fingers after the word to leave a space between this and the next one.

Where Do I Find the Strategies I Need?

When speaking to teachers at workshops or conferences, I often get asked, "So, Jen, can you just give us a list of the strategies we need to teach?"

Here's the thing: there really is no list of *the* strategies. Most of the ones I teach kids, I make up. That's right—they didn't come from a teacher's guide or discrete source. I made them up by reflecting on my own processes as a reader or writer and articulating them as a series of steps.

As Afflerbach, Pearson, and Paris (2008) wrote: Skills are automatic processes, strategies are deliberately controlled. This means that to teach a student a skill that you already possess as a proficient reader/writer, you need to apply a bit of metacognition to articulate the steps. For some, this is easiest when we put ourselves in a situation of challenge. In working through the challenge, the underground, automatic skill becomes more visible. For example, to help a student who needs work decoding multisyllabic words, you could try to get through a science journal article that would have many opportunities for you to practice your own decoding.

When you make your own strategies, they will be authentic, in language you're comfortable with, and easier to demonstrate. You'll know what you meant. Sometimes when teachers borrow others' language, they find it hard to pull off, they stumble over their words, or the demonstration doesn't quite match what they said they were demonstrating.

Resources for finding strategies for reading and writing instruction:

- *Already Ready* (Ray and Glover 2008)

- *In Pictures and In Words* (Ray 2010)

- *First Grade Readers* (Parsons 2010)

- *First Grade Writers* (Parsons 2005)

- *Second Grade Writers* (Parsons 2007)

- *Reading for Real* (Collins 2008)

- *Growing Readers* (Collins 2004)

- *How's It Going?* (Anderson 2000)

- *Invitations* (Routman 1994)

- *On Solid Ground* (Taberski 2000)

- *Units of Study in Opinion, Information, and Narrative Writing* (Calkins and colleagues 2013)

- *Curricular Plans for the Reading and Writing Workshop, Grades K–8* (Calkins and colleagues 2011)

- *Teaching Reading in Small Groups* (Serravallo 2010)

- *Independent Reading Assessment: Fiction* (Serravallo 2012)

- *Independent Reading Assessment: Nonfiction* (Serravallo 2013)

- *Conferring with Readers* (Serravallo and Goldberg 2007

Although my first answer is always to reflect and make your own for the reasons above, it is true that you can go to a number of resources to find sample strategies (see page 120). I would caution against using these as merely *the list* and instead think of them as a bank of examples.

Before rushing to one of those resources, try developing your own strategies by reflecting on your own reading. In the activity that follows, I'm going to ask you to read a high-level story to help you monitor your own comprehension. The strategies this exercise yields may not necessarily help you with teaching kindergarten and first-grade readers; the point of the exercise is to experience the mind work necessary to uncover what it is you do when you read and to practice developing strategies in your own words.

Read "The Real Princess," the short story by Hans Christian Anderson, in Figure 4.1. As you read, try to think about the characters in the story. Notice what you do to develop those ideas and thoughts.

The Real Princess
by Hans Christian Anderson

There was once a Prince who wished to marry a Princess; but then she must be a real Princess. He travelled all over the world in hopes of finding such a lady; but there was always something wrong. Princesses he found in plenty; but whether they were real Princesses it was impossible for him to decide, for now one thing, now another, seemed to him not quite right about the ladies. At last he returned to his palace quite cast down, because he wished so much to have a real Princess for his wife.

One evening a fearful tempest arose, it thundered and lightened, and the rain poured down from the sky in torrents: besides, it was as dark as pitch. All at once there was heard a violent knocking at the door, and the old King, the Prince's father, went out himself to open it.

It was a Princess who was standing outside the door. What with the rain and the wind, she was in a sad condition; the water trickled down from her hair, and her clothes clung to her body. She said she was a real Princess.

"Ah! We shall soon see that!" thought the old Queen-mother; however, she said not a word of what she was going to do; but went quietly into the bedroom, took all the bed-clothes off the bed, and put three little peas on the bedstead. She then laid twenty mattresses one upon another over the three peas, and put twenty feather beds over the mattresses.

Figure 4.1

continues

Upon this bed the Princess was to pass the night.

The next morning she was asked how she had slept. "Oh, very badly indeed!" she replied. "I have scarcely closed my eyes the whole night through. I do not know what was in my bed, but I had something hard under me, and am all over black and blue. It has hurt me so much!"

Now it was plain that the lady must be a real Princess, since she had been able to feel the three little peas through the twenty mattresses and twenty feather beds. None but a real Princess could have had such a delicate sense of feeling.

The Prince accordingly made her his wife; being now convinced that he had found a real Princess. The three peas were however put into the cabinet of curiosities, where they are still to be seen, provided they are not lost.

Wasn't this a lady of real delicacy?

Stop and think: What ideas do you have about the Queen? How about the Princess? Perhaps you think that the Queen mother was the one in control in the family. Or maybe that the Prince was a spoiled brat, or perhaps that the Princess was innocent and naïve. Or any number of other potential thoughts and reactions.

Now, reflect on how it is that you came upon those ideas. If you had to articulate a process you went through, what would you say it is? Perhaps what you did was hone in on one piece of particularly compelling dialogue and/or action that really revealed something about the character. For example, when the Queen says, "Ah! We shall soon see that!" perhaps you thought, "She's so distrustful," and when she set up the mattress test perhaps you thought, "If the prince wants a princess so badly, why doesn't he do the test? I guess mom's in charge at that castle."

So, to develop a strategy, you now need to articulate your process in terms that are not specific to the story. Perhaps your strategy would be something like, "Notice a place where the character is speaking or acting. Think to yourself, what kind of person would speak like that? Act like that? Use character traits to describe your character."

A strategy for developing strategies:

1. Put yourself in a situation where you have the opportunity to practice the skill for which you're trying to develop a strategy.
2. Spy on yourself as you read and think.
3. Articulate what you did—your process—into a series of generalizable steps.

So . . . What's the Plan for Marelle?

Remember that Marelle's goal is working on *structure/organization* in writing and on *retelling/sequencing* in reading.

Some of the skills she'll work to develop are:

- planning a beginning, middle, and end of a whole story
- retelling
- sequencing
- determining importance

Keep in mind that she'll be working on this goal for a while. Over the course of the next few weeks, I'll introduce strategies that I think best fit where she is in the journey toward reaching her goal and ones that best match the reading and writing units of study going on in the classroom. Some of the strategies I might teach her are:

- Plan a story by touching each page of a three-page booklet. Think about what happens first, next, and finally.
- Touch each page as you retell a story. Think about the most important thing that happens in the beginning, middle, and end of a book.
- Think about the problem the character is having and how the character solves her problem.

- Think about the main action in your story. Begin your story with what happened *right* before, and end your story with what happened *right* after.
- Retell your story across your hand, touching each finger and saying, "First, next, then, and then, finally."
- Act out your story with a partner and then retell what you just acted out.

ACTION →

Think about the goal you have for Emre or your chosen student. Identify the skills that will help him accomplish the goal. Brainstorm a few strategies that will help the student access those goals. My thoughts on Emre are in Appendix A.

Planning for Practice Over Time: Instructional Formats and Methods

For a student to accomplish a goal, she needs repeated practice with skills and strategies and a decreased level of support over time. One role of the teacher is to constantly assess where the student is in relation to the goal and to provide instruction that stretches, but doesn't overwhelm, the student. Working within the student's zone of proximal development ensures that your teaching is consistently building on a strength as opposed to teaching to a deficit (Vygotsky 1978).

If the strategy offered to the student, and the work required of the student, is a stretch beyond what he is already doing, chances are good the student will need some support. Scaffolding, a term first used in developmental literature by Wood, Bruner, and Ross (1976), was later applied to educational contexts to refer to the support a teacher provides to a student learning a new competency.

Like the scaffolds around a building under construction, instructional scaffolds are temporary and need to be removed over time. This gradual release of responsibility is often accomplished by choosing instructional formats and methods that at first offer the student a great deal of support and then over time expect that the student takes on more of the work with less and less teacher input (Pearson and Gallagher 1983). See Figure 4.2.

Instructional Formats and Degrees of Support

High	Moderate	Low
Minilesson	Shared reading	Independent reading
Interactive read-aloud	Strategy lessons	Partnerships
Close reading	Conferring	Peer editing
	Guided reading	
	Interactive writing	
	Shared writing	

Figure 4.2

On a microlevel, we can also study how we interact with students *within* each instructional format. For example, it's possible to teach a read-aloud that has a great deal of support—with the teacher doing a lot of thinking aloud, stopping often to prompt student thinking with a lot of support, offering opportunities for students to converse as they make sense of the text—as well as little support—reading a story straight through without stopping.

In *Teaching Reading in Small Groups* (2010), I wrote about the value of considering how much support you offer students before, during, and after a small-group lesson. Before, for example, you have the option to demonstrate, give an example, or just offer the strategy. During the guided practice, you can offer each student a range of support from elaborate prompts that offer a lot of support to nonverbal cues that put more responsibility on the student (see Figure 4.3).

Fisher and Frey, in their 2008 book *Better Learning through Structured Teaching*, offer a helpful diagram to conceptualize the gradually diminishing role of the teacher and the increased role of the student (see Figure 4.4).

In the sections that follow, I offer a brief description of some instructional formats that you may choose to use as you go about planning for instruction over time with your student. I will review structures that I use most often when working with students individually or in small groups. I have chosen not to describe whole-class teaching structures;

Three Levels of Decision Making to Move Children Toward Independence

Before Coached Practice	During Coached Practice	Over Time
What method will you use?	How supportive will your prompts be?	• How many times will you see the readers in the group?
• Demonstration		
	• Heavy	• How will you use leaner supports over time?
• Shared practice		
	• Medium	
• Example/explanation		• How will you support transference to new books?
	• Lean	
• State strategy		

Figure 4.3

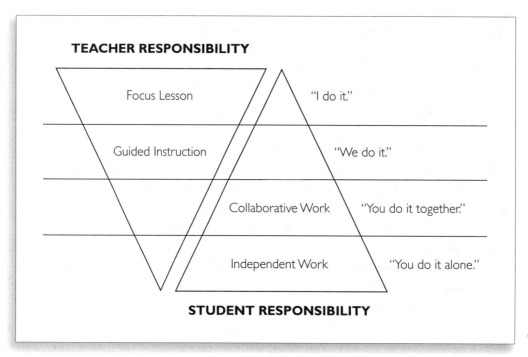

Figure 4.4 Over time, teachers should work to lessen their level of support and require more independence from the student. Different instructional formats can be chosen purposefully to offer varying levels of support.

however, minilessons and read-alouds would be excellent choices if you find that most of your class need the same work as the student you're currently focusing on. The methods I describe in this chapter are:

- Conferences (Research-Decide-Teach and Coaching)
- Small-Group Strategy Lessons
- Reading Partnerships and Reading Clubs: Conferring During Talk
- Writing Partnerships
- Shared Reading
- Shared Writing
- Interactive Writing
- Guided Reading

Keep in mind your goal of releasing responsibility over to the student by choosing structures that offer the most amount of support initially and then easing into structures that require the least amount of support gradually. In addition, keep in mind that you can vary your level of support within the lesson based on how near the student is to accomplishing the goal.

At the end of this chapter, I'll show how I would decide which of these formats to use with Marelle and how I would plan to use them over time.

Conferring

Individual conferences offer the opportunity for a teacher to sit with a student to learn about him, establish and follow-up on goals, hold him accountable for prior work, and offer guided practice with current work.

Within a reading workshop, students are reading different self-selected books at different reading levels. During writing workshop, students are writing their own pieces on different topics. Conferring allows me to see each student as an individual learner and teach each child strategies that best match her. The strategies I choose to teach are aligned to the goal I've chosen, and the level of support I provide during the conference matches where the child is in her own progress toward independent practice of the goal.

Most conferences follow a predictable structure that allows me as the teacher to make effective use of my time—both within the single conference, and across my entire class. If I spend too long with one student, offering a high level of support, not only have I spent time working on something the student will need me to be present for to continue practice, but the other students in the class have been robbed of instructional time. Without being too strict, I try to keep my eye on the clock and aim for a conference to last no more than about five minutes. Some will be a little shorter, some a little longer, but on average five minutes is what I'm aiming for.

The structure I find that I use most with students by the end of first, beginning of second grade is known as the "research-decide-teach" conference (Calkins 2000; Anderson 2000; Calkins, Hartman, and White 2005; Serravallo and Goldberg 2007). Using this structure, I'll first attempt to learn about what strategies the student is currently using and needs to learn and I'll choose a compliment and teaching point. Next, I'll articulate a clear compliment to reinforce a strength. Then, I'll state a strategy and support the student in practicing the strategy. Finally, I'll wrap up by reminding the student of my expectations for his continued work.

....

STRUCTURE OF A RESEARCH-DECIDE-TEACH CONFERENCE:

Research: Ask questions, observe, listen to the child read, investigate artifacts (such as sticky notes or reading logs). Keeping in mind the goal you've established and all you already know about the reader, notice how the student's current work reflects your prior assessments and the goal you established. Plan to spend about one minute of the five researching.

Decide: Decide on a compliment and teaching point. Ideally the compliment will segue to the teaching point. This will ensure that you're teaching to strengthen a strength as opposed to responding to a perceived deficit.

Compliment: Offer the student a clear, explicit compliment. Being as specific as possible, tell the student what he has done well and *why* it's important and offer an *example* of what he did that shows evidence of the strength. Being specific and elaborate with your compliment will ensure that the student can replicate the skill or behavior—which is sometimes something he didn't even realize he was doing.

Teach: Offer the student a specific strategy that he can practice to take the next step beyond what he is already doing. Say the strategy in clear, specific language. Depending on how much support the student needs, you may choose to give an example or offer a brief demonstration. Give the student a chance to practice with your support, as needed. Offer coaching prompts and questions. This is the longest part of the conference, lasting about two to three minutes.

Link: Repeat your teaching from today's conference, referring to how the work of today relates to the overarching goal you've established. At this point in the conference, I often find it helpful to establish a clear expectation for follow-up. I clarify what I expect the student to do before our next meeting and often give the student a tangible reminder of the strategy. Often I'll record the teaching point on a sticky note, a bookmark, or on a page of the student's reading or writing notebook. This will be quick—less than a minute.

Another common conferring structure for students in the primary grades is the coaching conference. Unlike a research, decide, teach conference where I begin with a minute or two of research, in a coaching conference I often know what I want to teach and I begin the conference by establishing the focus. This way, almost all of the four to five minutes can be used giving feedback to the student as he reads.

One reason coaching conferences are more common for primary-grade readers than upper-grade readers is that goals around print work and fluency are more common in grades K–2. I will get the most mileage coaching a student as she reads aloud. In a coaching conference, the student reads and I offer feedback while she is in the midst of the reading.

....

STRUCTURE OF A COACHING CONFERENCE:

Establish a focus/state a teaching point: Based on your prior conferences, or small groups, remind the student what she's been working on. Repeat the strategy or offer a new one aligned to the same goal.

Coach as the student reads: Ask the student to begin reading. Offer feedback as the student is reading. Try to *catch* the student both in times of success (in which case offer clear, explicit compliments) as well as in times of struggle (in which case offer support in the form of prompts, questions, and/or redirections).

Link: Repeat in clear language the work that you did together today and encourage the child to continue practicing. Leave a tangible reminder—such as a bookmark or sticky note—to support his ongoing independent practice.

Small-Group Strategy Lessons

In *Teaching Reading in Small Groups* (2010) I explore more than a dozen types of small-group instruction formats that may be chosen as an alternative to guided reading to match the myriad purposes that arise in a given classroom. Perhaps the most common and versatile of these is the small-group strategy lesson. They are versatile because I can use them in reading or writing, for any skill or behavior that I want to reinforce.

Strategy lessons offer an opportunity for students to practice new strategies or review strategies they've learned before. During the small-group lessons, the students will all practice the same strategy while the teacher moves around supporting each individual student at his entry point. It is for this reason that I also refer to strategy lessons as *group conferences*—I try to maintain the same individualized feel as a one-on-one conference.

Strategy lessons, like all the other structures I mention in this chapter, follow a predictable framework that will help teachers to plan, help children to know their responsibilities, and allow everyone to make the best use of time during the lesson.

While the other students are reading or writing independently, I begin the lesson by establishing the focus for our seven to ten minutes together. I state the strategy in clear language and offer a visual (chart or icons) if I think it would support the students. I try to get students working as quickly as possible—within ninety seconds or so—and then begin to make my way around the group. Like a plate spinner in the circus, trying to keep plates up on the end of sticks before they drop, I try to keep each student working productively as I move quickly among them. As I move from student to student, I offer feedback and support to appropriately nudge each student toward independent practice of the strategy. At the end, I repeat the strategy either as a whole group or on an individual basis.

....

STRATEGY LESSON STRUCTURE:

Connect and compliment: Begin the lesson by establishing a clear purpose and a connection to the ongoing work of the students' goal. This is a great time to remind students of their goal and/or to remind them how the work they will do in reading relates to writing or vice versa. Whenever possible, I also try to offer a compliment to reinforce a common strength. Keep this quick—about thirty seconds.

Teach: After a quick introduction, I state the teaching point, or strategy, for today's lesson. Depending on how new the strategy is, I'll decide on the level of upfront support. For example, if this is the first time they've heard the strategy, it's likely I'll provide a brief demonstration where I'll read or write as well as model my thinking. If they've tried the strategy before, I may offer less support in the form of a quick example or explanation. If this is a strategy that the children have practiced many times before, I'll probably just state the strategy and then get them working right away.

Actively engage: By now, the lesson is about ninety seconds in. I'm now going to offer differentiated, individualized support as I move from student to student in the group. Spending thirty to sixty seconds with each student, I make my way around, coaching as they practice. I'll often quickly assess and then offer feedback in the form of prompts. Prompts may be questions, directives, redirections, or compliments.

Link: Before students return to independent reading or writing, I want to send the message that they should continue practicing without my support until we meet again. I'll either speak to each student individually or I'll call all of the students' attention back together. I'll choose the individual route if I tweaked the teaching point for individuals during the active engagement section. If the coaching support I provided was pretty consistent across students, I'll repeat the teaching point to all of them. As in a conference, here is where I'll often tell students what I expect for them to do between now and when I see them again, and I'll often give the students some sort of a tangible reminder to focus them as they continue to practice on their own. This is a quick wrap-up, lasting less than a minute.

Reading Partnerships and Reading Clubs: Conferring During Talk

Partnerships and reading clubs offer young readers experience with an essential ingredient to being an engaged, lifelong reader: the ability to have social interactions around books.

In primary classrooms where students are reading very short texts and stamina may be a challenge, partnerships also offer the ability to vary the energy in the room to help readers read for longer periods of time. For instance, instead of readers sitting alone, reading independently for thirty minutes, a teacher may choose to ask students to read independently for ten, with a partner for ten, and then independently again for ten. As students become more practiced with working in partnerships, teachers may choose to move to reading clubs, like those described by Collins (2008) in *Reading for Real.*

Even the youngest children can also be taught how to talk about books. Great conversations can invigorate children, spark new thinking, and encourage laughter. They can help students to come to new insights and even increase motivation to read (Collins 2008).

Whether students are sitting side by side with one book between them, talking about the thoughts and ideas from their own books, or working in reading clubs, students can benefit from some instruction (Collins 2008; Serravallo 2010; Nichols 2006; Calkins 2000). Children need to learn how to work together to be productive, practicing the same skills and strategies they are expected to practice when they read alone. Many need to learn how to have a conversation, period, and then when the talk is focused on books, a child's comprehension (or lack thereof) also comes into play.

While students work with their partner or club either reading together or talking about their books, the teacher often circulates around the room, offering suggestions to each group. These are opportunities to confer. And, because there are two children working together, you can think of it as a ready-made small group!

When conferring during partnerships or reading clubs, my conference tends to follow a predictable structure. When I first arrive to where a partnership of students is working together, I listen to them read and/or talk without interrupting to ask my own questions. I stay on the periphery, taking notes in the form of a quick transcript. As I write, I'm thinking about a compliment—something they are doing well that I'll want to reinforce—and a teaching point—some way to stretch their work. Sometimes what I choose to teach has to do with behaviors, other times comprehension, other times conversation. Still other times, I'll think about the goals I have for them that pertain to the level of text that they are reading and I'll support them in doing the work I'm asking them to do independently, now and with the support of a partner (Serravallo 2010).

When I've decided what to teach, I'll use one of four methods: ghost partner, proficient partner, example and explanation, or demonstration.

- With ghost partner, I'll whisper prompts and sentence starters into the students' ears, encouraging them to reuse my language with the club. All of the prompts I whisper will focus on a specific teaching point.
- With proficient partner, I'll join the club or partnership offering ideas and questions to keep the conversation going.
- With example and explanation or demonstration, I treat it more like a strategy lesson—interrupting the partnership or club to state a clear teaching point and showing them what I mean. In all instances, I'll wrap up by repeating my teaching with a link.

Regardless of whether I choose ghost partner, proficient partner, example and explanation, or demonstration, I find that my overall structure stays the same. These methods are folded into the *teach* section of the conference.

A SUGGESTED STRUCTURE FOR CONFERRING DURING CONVERSATION:

Research: Listen to student conversation, or the students working together to read the text, without interrupting. Although I may have questions in my mind that beg for clarification, I try to only go on what I'm hearing the students say. Interrupting them to ask questions will disrupt the flow of conversation.

Decide: As I listen, I am trying to decide on a teaching point. I think about conversational skills, comprehension skills, and/or level-specific reading behaviors that I'll want to support. As with any type of conferring, I'm looking to strengthen strengths, not teach to deficits. I keep the students' goals in mind as I select a teaching point.

Teach: I chose one of four methods: ghost partner, proficient partner, example and explanation, or demonstration. Staying focused on just one strategy, I'll either coach by whispering in the student's ears, joining the conversation, or showing and telling the strategy.

Link: Before leaving the group to continue talking without me there, I'll repeat the teaching point for today's lesson. I'll establish accountability by reminding them that I'll look for their practice the next time I see them.

Writing Partnerships

In her 2004 book *Independent Writing*, M. Colleen Cruz talks about the importance of community to a developing writer. Writers need other writers who know their struggles and triumphs and can support them along all steps of the writing process. Writing partners can help each other along all steps of the writing process as they critique, compliment, and offer advice and support.

In many classrooms I visit, teachers have paired students up as writing partners with good intentions. But sometimes, feeling the pressure of so much to cover in so little time, teachers only have students meet once in a while—usually at the end of the process, for peer editing. But as Cruz reminds us, there is so much more that can happen during these writing groups. When a student's goal involves anything including doing more planning before writing, being more intentioned and purposeful about revision, or studying mentor authors to improve craft, doing more during partnership time can be another great source of support for the writer.

These partnerships can be permanent or temporary arrangements. Students will need to prepare for their work together by bringing a sample of their writing to share, a question they want answered, and/or an intention to do some out-loud planning. The first student might read aloud the whole piece or a part of the piece and then ask for feedback. Or, the writer can decide to pose a problem to the partner, then read the writing and hear suggestions. Students can also rehearse orally, storytelling aloud and getting help from a peer.

Teachers can play an important role in partnership meetings by helping students to ask probing questions and teaching them how to offer criticism that is constructive. Teachers may also help to focus students on their particular goal and help them to craft questions that will help lend insight toward improvement with that goal. When I'm working with a writing partnership, I tend to follow the same structure as that during a reading partnership. That is, I research by observing, I choose something to teach, then I use one of the conferring into conversation teaching methods described on page 133. As with all teaching, I'll wrap up with a link to make sure that the teaching I've done can transfer to new contexts and new pieces of writing.

Shared Reading

Shared reading is a method developed by Donald Holdaway (1984) and written about by Brenda Parkes (2000), Sarah Daunis and Maria Iams (2007), and others. In primary elementary classrooms, shared reading is most commonly done as a whole class, though it also can be done in a small group.

One essential element of shared reading is that everyone is reading together from the same physical copy of a text—a big book, a chart, a poster, or an overhead projection. The teacher is able to hold the students' attention to the same point in the text and take advantage of direct instruction teaching opportunities and opportunities to give children feedback while they are in the midst of reading.

During a shared reading lesson, whether whole class or small group, the whole class usually reads the text in unison, chorally, while the teacher points underneath the words or at the start of the line to keep the class together. The children benefit from hearing the other readers—peers or me—around them reading while they do. When and if the students become disfluent, have difficulty figuring out a word, or stumble through a portion of the text, I may stop and use that teachable moment to provide support with print work or fluency instruction.

Ideally, the text that is chosen, according to Brenda Parkes (2000), should be slightly above the level of the highest reader. Pulling students together who read at about the same reading level into a small group can allow the teacher to select a text that affords them some challenges without so much difficulty that they can't participate or would become frustrated when doing so.

My shared reading lessons often follow a predictable structure. I begin by stating the intention for the group, based on their goals. I support the students as they read in chorus and offer feedback and strategies as they read. I both maintain my planned lesson focus and allow myself to respond to teachable moments.

....

SHARED READING STRUCTURE:

Connect: Gather students and begin by telling them why they have been pulled together. Often, I compliment a strength I've seen in their reading, then segue to the teaching I've chosen for the group.

Teach: Offer a strategy in clear and explicit language.

Read with feedback: The children will now begin reading in chorus. I might read with the students (if they benefit from a little extra support), or my voice might drop out to decrease scaffolding and to better hear what the children can and can't do without my support. As the children read, I offer coaching tips, suggestions, directives, and compliments. Some of these may be planned opportunities, others may come up in the midst of the lesson.

Link: At the end of the lesson, I recap what we worked on together. I again state the strategy clearly and in the same language, and strongly urge the children to continue practice in their own books back at their seats.

Shared Writing

Shared writing is a structure used to help students experience the process writers can go through to compose a text—from planning, to drafting, to revising and editing. In shared writing, the teacher leads the students through the process, scaffolding students' use of language, either writing one piece together as a class, working with small groups or partnerships, or, in some cases, working with individual students. The teacher uses the students' suggestions for what to write down, although the teacher is the only one who does any writing and some of the language conventions may be revised from the child's initial suggestion to the actual writing down of the text.

During a shared writing lesson, you can support students in composing a great deal of text because you are able to write much more quickly. Shared writing is a great choice for students whose goals center around overall structure, like Marelle, or for students who would benefit from support with writing process. It may also be a great choice for students who are just moving into levels A and B: the teacher could write a patterned multi-page book with a group, then make mini-copies for them to keep and reread as they practice reading left to right across the page, and work on following a pattern and one-to-one matching.

Shared writing is a great choice for students whose goals center around overall structure, or for students who would benefit from support with writing process.

During a shared writing lesson, the teacher and students may compose a whole or part of a text. Therefore, the structure of the lesson may vary somewhat. If the class is beginning a new text together, the teacher may lead the students in conversation (often by posing a question and having students turn and talk with a partner before sharing out to the group) about what they'll write about. For example, if the teacher is trying to show how to write an opinion piece because the class has never tried this type of writing before, the teacher may say, "Today we're going to write to try to convince someone of something. We'll write a letter and share our thoughts on something important. Let's think together first. What's something this whole class really cares about? What's something we want to see change? Turn and talk with your partner."

A topic you select will have to be common knowledge among all of the students in the class or group, because they'll all have a hand in composing it. Once a topic is decided upon, a teacher will usually then lead the students in planning what the piece will say, possibly tucking in some advice that can be transferred to their own writing—for example, "Great idea to write a letter to our principal asking for more books for our hamster center. We are going to have to work hard to convince her because I'm not sure she'll see it like we do. What are some reasons we can give her to convince her? Turn and talk with your partner." When a student volunteers with "So that we can give it food" the teacher might rephrase to "Oh, we so we should write, 'We need to know what to feed our hamster. We can learn that from a book,'" so that the writing is conventionally correct and makes sense.

As the teacher is writing the words on the page, he may involve the students in brief ways. For example, she might say, "Hmm. *What.* We know that word. It's on our word wall, right? Can everyone turn and find it. What letter is it under? Will you spell it out loud for me as I write it quickly on the page?"

Through choosing a topic, planning, sketching, writing, and revising and editing, the teacher is supporting the students' sense of writing process and language.

....

SHARED WRITING STRUCTURE:

Plan: The teacher leads the students in conversation to plan what they will write. Often the students will turn and talk with a partner as the teacher listens in, coaching students' use of language and understandings of the conventions of the genre of text they're writing.

Write: After planning out the whole text, the teacher will lead the students to go back to the beginning, and decide what to write first. The teacher can take a suggestion from a student (rephrasing as necessary to make sure it makes sense and is grammatically correct), or can listen in and say "I heard . . . ." The teacher quickly records what was planned and then moves on to the next part or page of the writing, again eliciting student involvement in the composition of the text. Another day, the teacher might involve the students in shared practice with another step of the writing process—planning out the writing in pictures, editing, and/or revising.

Link: The teacher ends the lesson by reminding students of a takeaway from their shared practice—such as making sure the pictures they drew to plan the story match the words on each page of the story.

Interactive Writing

Interactive writing has some similarities to shared writing. Like shared writing, the teacher leads the writers through the process to compose a coherent text. One important difference, however, is that the teacher and student *share* the pen. In this way, the children participate to a greater degree (McCarrier, Pinnell, and Fountas 1999).

In an interactive writing lesson, the whole class or a group of children gather with the teacher. They begin by deciding what they'll write about and plan out how they'll write it. The pacing of these lessons is slow and deliberate, so the amount of text should be limited. For example, an appropriate amount of writing might be a shopping list for what to get for the new class pet, a brief invitation to the principal to join this Friday's writing celebration, or a sign for the classroom door asking passersbys to please keep their voices down as kids are thinking inside.

After deciding what they'll write, the teacher guides the students in composing the text. The teacher may involve the students in a variety of practices helpful to beginning writers, including:

- saying a sentence and counting how many words they plan to write, then writing lines on the paper to represent one written word for each spoken word
- saying a word slowly to hear all the sounds, then checking the alphabet chart to decide what letter to write to represent the sound they hear
- checking the word wall for a high-frequency word and writing that word quickly
- rereading what has been written so far, making sure they haven't left any words out, and pointing under each word as they reread
- forming letters properly
- revising/editing when a mistake is made, for example, using a capital letter instead of a lowercase letter when writing someone's name
- discussing and deciding on ending punctuation

As the teacher involves students in the aforementioned practices, typically one student at a time will be chosen to come up to the chart or easel or SMART Board and write while the rest of the class writes on a personal whiteboard or pretends to write by using their finger on the carpet, using their neighbor's back, using the palm of their hand, or writing in the air.

Because the text will be something that is hung in the classroom as a model, and possibly read and reread several times, it's important that the resulting writing is conventionally correct. Teachers will often use white tape or a piece of a white label to cover up mistakes and support students as they make corrections right on the text. The resulting text will have a variety of types of handwriting, as in Figure 4.5.

Interactive writing is often most effective and commonly used in kindergarten classrooms or in classrooms with large amounts of emergent or beginning readers. As with shared writing, completed pieces of interactive writing can be duplicated and given to students working on A/B-level behaviors such as one-to-one matching and moving left to right across the page.

Figure 4.5 A sample of interactive writing from Kristine Mraz's kindergarten class. Notice that the teacher writes some words/letters ("EVERY TIME") and students write some ("spritz").

INTERACTIVE WRITING STRUCTURE:

Plan: The teacher leads the students in conversation to plan what they will write.

Compose: With support from the teacher, the students go word by word, working with resources in the room to write the words. Students are called upon to write various parts of the word (onset, rime, initial letter, and so on) and/or an entire word (such as a word from the word wall, a classmate's name that is posted in the class on a chart). While one student is up at the chart or easel writing, the teacher is simultaneously helping him *and* is involving the children in their own practice with writing the letter(s) or word on whiteboard or invisibly with their finger.

Link: The teacher ends the lesson reminding the students of a takeaway from their shared practice—such as the value of using the word wall to help spell words or the importance of saying a word slowly to hear all the sounds before writing the word down on the page.

Guided Reading

Guided reading is a small-group structure used to support students' reading of instructional-level texts. In a guided reading lesson, the teacher pulls together a group of readers who read at the same level with, ideally, the same types of needs. She carefully selects a text that is at their instructional level (one that can be read with 90 to 95 percent accuracy, or one where fluency or comprehension is less than secure). It's important that the text offers students the right balance of supports and challenges.

Because the book is too hard for students to read independently, the teacher's role in providing appropriate support is crucial. The teacher will need to plan a *text introduction* that helps to activate prior knowledge, support students with text structure, introduce key vocabulary words, and set an intention for reading. In the words of Fountas and Pinnell, authors of the book *Guided Reading* (1996), the introduction needs to "keep in mind the meaning, language, and visual information of the book and the knowledge, experience, and skills of the reader" (7).

Students then read independently as the teacher circulates among them listening to them read and prompting and offering support. After the reading, the teacher may offer a new strategy and/or discuss the content of the text with the students.

....

GUIDED READING LESSON STRUCTURE:

Book/text introduction: The teacher, using a plan made while considering the students in the group, introduces some of the challenges of the text while leaving some for the students to work through during the reading. Aspects of the introduction may include any or all of the following: activating the readers' prior knowledge, offering main plot points, summarizing a main idea, introducing unfamiliar text structures, showing and defining challenging vocabulary, teaching a word feature that will show up often in the book (i.e., -*ing*), and/or offering a focus question or strategy.

Reading with coaching: Students read independently, whisper reading at lower levels and reading silently at higher levels. The teacher makes her way around to each student and listens to the student read. During times of challenge, the teacher offers supportive prompts and questions. When the student overcomes a challenge, the teacher may compliment by naming what the student has done.

Discussion and teaching: After all children have read the selected text at least once (at lower levels students will often reread and at higher levels students will often be reading only a portion of a longer text), the teacher will call the students back together to offer a teaching point based on her observations and/or will engage the children in a discussion about the text.

Link The teacher repeats some main takeaways from today's lesson. Students typically will keep the book used during guided reading to reread, practicing increased fluency, accuracy, and comprehension.

So . . . What's the Plan for Marelle?

In reading workshop, I would plan to work with Marelle in both guided reading lessons and strategy lessons. Because her running record shows that she could use some support at her independent level, I'd begin working with her for a few weeks at level F in strategy lessons. I'd introduce some retelling strategies to her and a couple of her peers who could also benefit from the instruction.

After a few weeks, I'd hope that Marelle's work in books at level F is significantly stronger. At that point, I'd begin introducing level G in guided reading lessons, choosing books that have a clear plot structure to support her retelling work and grouping her with other students who are also ready to transition to books at level G.

During the week or two when she's working in guided reading at level G, I'll also continue working with her at level F (and the G books from guided reading that she's rereading), repeating opportunities for guided practice with the same retelling strategies and helping her apply them to new books. I'll also check in with her and her partner during partnership time to make sure they are spending some of their time together retelling.

While she works on her goal, I'm going to support Marelle in choosing only narratives from the classroom library.

During writing workshop, I'll work with Marelle during her partnership time to help her use the process of planning a beginning, middle, and end across a three-page booklet. I'll teach her partner to prompt her to make sure that each event that she plans to put on each page connects and are in sequence.

I'll also work with Marelle and some other students in the class in shared writing lessons, planning and writing stories with clear structure and transitions between pages.

> **ACTION** ➡️
>
> Consider Emre or the student from your class you've chosen to make a plan for. Which of the instructional formats described in this chapter might be a good fit for him? Think about the purposes of each when making your decision. Jot down some plans.

⬜ Practice Over Time: Involving Others

One of the most significant hurdles to making timely progress with a goal is when the work a student is told to do, and/or the teaching she receives, is muddled and confused. When a student receives mixed messages about what to be focusing on, the end result is often that the child focuses on none of it.

Students who qualify for intervention are often the students who are most vulnerable to this confusion. These students are pulled out during class time or work with specialists who *push in* during literacy periods. In either case, these interventionists often have made their own plans for the student. By virtue of the fact that a teacher's day is overscheduled and busy as it is, these interventionists and classroom teachers rarely have time to sit down with each other. Although it may be true that everything each teacher teaches is helpful to the student, it's probably also true that focusing on the most important work and being a united front will yield faster progress and less confusion on the part of the learner.

Acknowledging teachers' workloads are only becoming greater, there may be ways to put systems in place to communicate among the adults involved that won't require extra work. A few ideas are to have a communication sheet with a goal at the top of the page and places to add strategies and tools, as well as ongoing note taking (see Figure 4.6).

Within the school, this can be kept in a two-pocket folder by the front door of the classroom in a basket. Whenever a reading specialist or English-as-a-second-language teacher comes to pick up a student for intervention, the routine could be that he takes the folder with him, reviews the most current strategies taught and notes taken, and then teaches in a way that aligns to the message the student has already been getting within the classroom. Then, at the end of the thirty-minute session, the reading specialist would also jot down his own notes about the student's work during that period and would return the folder to its spot by the door. If every classroom in a school had this sort of

Marelle

Name	W or R?	Date	Strengths	Teaching (today and going forward...)
Joan	W	6/12	-plans writing B· M	-ending relates to beginning
FJ	R	6/14	-retells story by touching pages	-try to retell some parts without looking back at pictures.
Joan	R	6/15	-retells beginning and middle from memory· uses picture for ending of story	-includes some events that are less important· Talked about problem-solution·

Figure 4.6 Note-Taking Form for Communicating with Other Teachers About Students' Goals (See Appendix C for blank version.)

system, the cross-classroom communication could be streamlined and a student could receive more consistent instruction.

Add this within-school challenge to the home–school connection challenge. At times, students go home to parents or caregivers who have different ideas about what good schoolwork looks like or what is most important to pay attention to. In one school where I taught for three years, most parents seemed very concerned with handwriting and spelling above all else. Although I agree it's important for children to learn proper letter formation and to spell in ways that allow their writing to be read by others, it was only in maybe one case where I would have agreed that those were the most important areas to focus on. So another question to consider is, "How will you make the student's goal clear to the adults the child goes home to each night?"

Teachers could also adopt a home–school connection system (see Figure 4.7). In my work in many different schools, I've seen different systems work well. In one school, the last page of the reading and writing notebooks are reserved for teaching notes. After a conference or small group, the student dates and records her own understanding of the teaching that took place during that lesson. Notebooks go home each night and parents could then see the teaching that's happening.

To many parents, reading and writing workshops feel hard to understand because there is no textbook and there are no tests. Because of this, many parents can feel disconnected from the curriculum and the individualized teaching that happens with their child in the classroom. Some system—in a notebook, on paper, through ongoing emails, or in-person conferences—can help parents to feel part of the process.

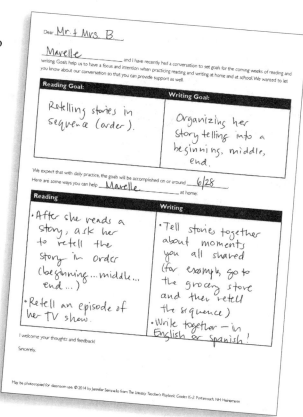

Figure 4.7 Communication with parents about a student's goals is crucial to ensure consistency between home and school.

So . . . What's the Plan for Marelle?

Marelle is an English language learner who works with a teacher who pushes into the classroom to support her. I want to be mindful that the support she receives is *in addition to*, and *not instead of*, independent reading and writing.

Therefore, if the teacher is pushing in during reading, I'd ask her to help Marelle retell with her partner after reading the story. If the teacher pushes in during writing, I'd ask her to support Marelle during partnership time planning out her story. If the teacher's time in the classroom significantly overlaps with the independent work time, I'd ask the teacher to take on some of the conferring and small-group work that I planned to do, so that Marelle isn't spending all of her practice time working with a teacher.

I would try, if at all possible, to see if the ESL teacher could work with Marelle and a few other students to do oral storytelling. This storytelling in a small group—either retelling a story of something that happened to all of them, such as a recent fire drill, or making up a story together—can help not only solidify their understanding of story structure, but could also help with what will likely be her next goal—elaboration.

Marelle's parents speak Spanish only. I would plan to involve them by getting help translating a letter informing them of what Marelle will be working on with her teachers in school. I'll encourage them to practice some of the same things at home in Spanish. For example, after watching a show together, they can turn off the TV and retell what happened in sequence. When they are driving in a car together, they can make up a story.

ACTION →

Make plans for involving others in Emre's plans or the plans of the student you've chosen from your class.

Practice Over Time: Planning for Multiple Students and Across a Week

For several weeks ahead, you and each of your students will meet in a variety of instructional formats. As you meet, you'll be introducing new strategies when needed.

I find that typically a student will need a few opportunities of guided practice with a strategy. This guided practice could be in a conference, in a small group, or during a partnership or other structure. When a student *gets it* the very first time I teach it, I usually feel that the teaching might not have reached far enough.

Once a student develops a level of automaticity with a strategy, I'll introduce a new strategy—still keeping in mind the focus of the goal we've established. For example, if Marelle starts to do well with a writing strategy of planning across three pages, then I might introduce an extra page or even two, and teach her how to go from just the beginning, middle, and end to more of a *first, next, then, and then, finally* structured story. Once she does well with that, then I might move on to a new strategy, perhaps asking her to think about her story as having a problem that the character will need to try to solve across three more pages and eventually solve on the last.

In other words, the strategies can build upon each other, each strategy offering a new level of depth.

Each week as you plan your whole-class, small-group, and individual instruction, it's a good idea to revisit any notes you took during your work with the student. Using these notes will help you to consider when to move on to new teaching and when to revisit a previously taught strategy.

Once you take the ideas in this book to scale and have a clearly set goal for each student in your class, you'll use this master class list of goals to help you decide on your approach for the week. To transfer a list of student names into a weekly plan, I typically start with groups, then individuals. Looking at my class list, I follow a process such as this:

1. I ask myself, "Which students have similar goals and are at a similar reading/writing level?" I then group those students and put them into the strategy lesson row, and put a check mark next to their names to indicate that I have a plan for them.
2. I ask myself, "Which students' goals lend themselves to work during partnership/club/conversation time?" and I plan to see them during the two to three days a week where I have set aside time during conversation.
3. I ask myself, "Which students have goals that are somewhat unique?" Those students are ones that I'll plan to see one-on-one in conferences.
4. I ask myself, "Whom should I be sure to check in with more than once?" and I'll make it a point to repeat a strategy lesson and/or conference or leave in buffer time for myself at the end of the workshop to observe or check in with students who may need added reminders or coaching.

In the example in Figure 4.8 you can see the class at a glance, and in Figure 4.9 you can see my plan for the week. Notice that I've grouped readers who have similar needs together in small groups. For example, Isabelle, Sasha, Elizabeth, Erin, and Mason are working on print work or fluency, so they'll be working together in small-group shared reading lessons. Rebecca and Selma, working at levels K and J respectively, are both working on synthesizing chapters in their early chapter books. They'll be together in a strategy lesson to support them with this goal. The plan in Figure 4.9 is for *reading* only. Another would need to be made for writing workshop time.

Figure 4.8 Each student in the class has one goal for reading. Including a column for the child's reading level allows you to ensure that you're grouping children who read at about the same level.

Class Profile

Levels and Goals (Reading)

NAME	LEVEL	GOAL AND NOTES
Allessandra	M	Inferring (character)
Melissa	L	vocabulary
Desiree	G	integrate sources of info.
Erin	G	fluency - intonation
Marelle	F	sequencing/retelling
Paul	K	vocabulary
Emre	L/M	char. analysis
Rebecca	K	synthesis
Mason	K	fluency - intonation
Allan	L	vocabulary
Pete	H	cause + effect, plot in sequence
Tripp	F	sequencing/retelling
Alice	H	↑ self-correction rate
Elizabeth	I	fluency - phrasing
Sasha	I	multi-syllabic word decoding
Isabelle	F	fluency - intonation
Jose	M	interpretation - lesson? message?
Selma	J	synthesis - connect chapters

Planning Your Week

	Monday	Tuesday	Wednesday	Thursday	Friday
Strategy Lesson (10 min)		Rebecca+ Selma (synthesis) ⑩			
Strategy Lesson (10 min) (small group SR)	Shared ⑩ reading - Isabelle Sasha Elizabeth Erin Mason		repeat ⑩ SR from Monday		repeat ⑩ SR from Monday
Conferences (5 minutes each)	Marelle ⑤	Tripp ⑤		Selma ⑤ Paul ⑤	Desiree ⑤
Guided Reading (15–20 min)		Pete, ⑮ Alice H→I		Pete, ⑮ Alice H→I	
Other (___10min) Partner/ Club Talk	Allessandra, Emre, Jose ⑩		Melissa+ Alan ⑤ (vocab)		
Notes	Extra Flex time	⑩	⑤	㉒	⑩	㉒

May be photocopied for classroom use. From The Literacy Teacher's Playbook: Grades K–2. Portsmouth, NH: Heinemann. © 2012 by Jennifer Serravallo.
from Independent Reading Assessment: Fiction, New York, NY: Scholastic, Inc.

Figure 4.9 This Planning Your Week template was used to plan thirty-five minutes of conferring, small-group instruction, and talk time. I plan to see every student in the class between one and three times in some format, and there is plenty of flextime built in for needs that arise during the workshop, or for when lessons need to be rescheduled. While students are working with the teacher individually or in a group, the rest of the class is reading independently. When the teacher is working with a partnership during talk time, the rest of the class is also discussing their books or reading with their partners.

ACTION →

Using the template in Appendix C, page 181, or one you
create yourself based on Figure 4.9, create a weekly plan
for your class. If you're working with Emre's data, you can
use Figure 4.8 to create an alternate weekly plan.

Knowing When the Goal Has Been Met

Ideally, this cycle of assessment, goal setting, and teaching will repeat many times
throughout the school year. But when will you know when it's time to go back to the
beginning of the cycle, look at fresh work, and set a new goal?

As important as it is to have a clear sense of what you want to work on, you also need
to know what it looks like when the work is done. The information in Chapter 2 may
be a help to you here. Look back at what made you identify the goal in the first place—
probably a gap between the work the student was currently doing and the *ideal* of what
work should look like.

You may also refer to your grade-level standards, rubrics, benchmarks, continuums,
and other tools that may provide an image for you of what a strong example of work
would be. Some resources for this include:

- *The Continuum of Literacy Learning* (Fountas and Pinnell 2010) offers guidance
  by Fountas and Pinnell, levels of the skills, and behaviors students should exhibit.
- *Units of Study in Opinion, Information, and Narrative Writing* (Calkins and
  colleagues 2013) offers student-facing and teacher-facing checklists and rubrics
  for what to look for in information, narrative, and opinion writing, as well as
  student exemplars
- *Independent Reading Assessment: Fiction* (Serravallo 2012) and *Independent
  Reading Assessment: Nonfiction* (Serravallo 2013) include a ladder of increasing expectations for student work by reading level, as well as rubrics with
  sample student responses and descriptors to better understand what it looks
  like when a student is showing strong comprehension at each level from K to
  W (fiction) and J to W (nonfiction).

Over the course of the year, a student's goals will shift and change. Reading levels will increase, and, with that, a student will be tasked with handling a new set of textual challenges. Keep in mind that children in grades K and 1 typically make much faster progress through reading levels than students in grades 2 and above, and your cycle of settling on a new goal should happen more frequently for younger children. Also, your curriculum will take you through narrative, informational, and opinion writing units and reading units of study focusing on narrative and informational texts.

A student's strengths and needs, therefore, will evolve as the curriculum and her development as a reader and writer do. One of the teacher's responsibilities is to constantly have his eyes open, looking for progress, and to know when it's time to reestablish a goal. See Figure 4.10 for an example of how Marelle's progress—and the monitoring of her progress—evolved across one year. You can keep track of this progress over time with a conferring notes system.

Marelle's Goal Setting and Progress Across a School Year

Month	Units of Study in Reading and Writing	Marelle's Progress
September	Readers Build Good Habits and Launching the Writer's Workshop (personal narrative)	9/20: Goal established—focus and stamina for reading and writing
October/November	Tackling Trouble (reading) and Writing for Readers	10/10: Integrating visual source of information when reading (level C) and recording more of the sounds she hears (writing)
November/December	Readers Meet Characters and Realistic Fiction	11/15: Holding on to meaning, not overrelying on visual; inferring feelings (reading) and showing character feeling in pictures (writing)

Figure 4.10

continues

Marelle's Goal Setting and Progress Across a School Year (cont.)

Month	Units of Study in Reading and Writing	Marelle's Progress
January	Nonfiction Reading and How-to Books	1/5: Fluency—phrasing two to three words at a time in reading; trying to write known words automatically (writing)
February/March	Tricky Words (revisited) and Opinion Writing: Letters	2/2: Using blends and common word endings in reading and writing (and connecting to word study)
March/April	Reading Like a Scientist and Information Books	3/15: Monitoring and self-correcting (reading), writing for readers and revision (writing)
May	Character Reading Clubs and Authors as Mentors	5/28: Retelling and sequencing (reading) and writing with clear story structure (writing)
June	Reading About Topics Across Genre: Information Books, Poetry, and Prose; Writing Poetry	6/20: To be determined

○ Wrap-Up

As you've worked through this book, I hope that you've been able to internalize the four-step process of collecting data, analyzing it, crafting goals, and creating an action plan that have the potential to impact your instruction and your students' learning. Working alongside my analysis and goal setting with Marelle, I hope that you've kept Emre's work by your side.

At this point, you can turn to your own students' work. Keep in mind, as I mentioned at the end of Chapter 2, that it's unlikely that you'll do this work for every student in your class right away. My hope is that you begin to take on this process with a select handful of students. Maybe those who puzzle you most—your most struggling, your highest achieving, the student who has been stuck for a while.

As you work to create goals for your students, I hope you've also created goals for yourself. What will you study? What will you read? What will you try?

Keep in mind that this work is never done. The rhythms of this type of data-informed teaching are much like the cycles of the football season. A teaching cycle ends with students reaching their goals; a football season ends (best-case scenario) with winning the Super Bowl. After celebrating, training for the next season starts up again. The team moves through training on the field, regular season games, and playoffs—and then on to another Super Bowl. In your classroom, throughout the year, you'll cycle through seasons of monitoring a student's progress, collecting new assessment data, making decisions, crafting a goal, working toward that goal, and, if all goes well, the student achieving that goal. We're lucky to work in a profession where our learning is never done; there is always a way to improve one's game, always a way to come up with new plays, new strategies to outgrow your best self—and, with the data on your side, to help your students do the same.

APPENDIX A

Emre's Work and One Possible Interpretation

Figures A.1–A.7 are available to download at www.heinemann.com/products/E05300.aspx (click on the Companion Resources tab).

Step 1: Collect Data

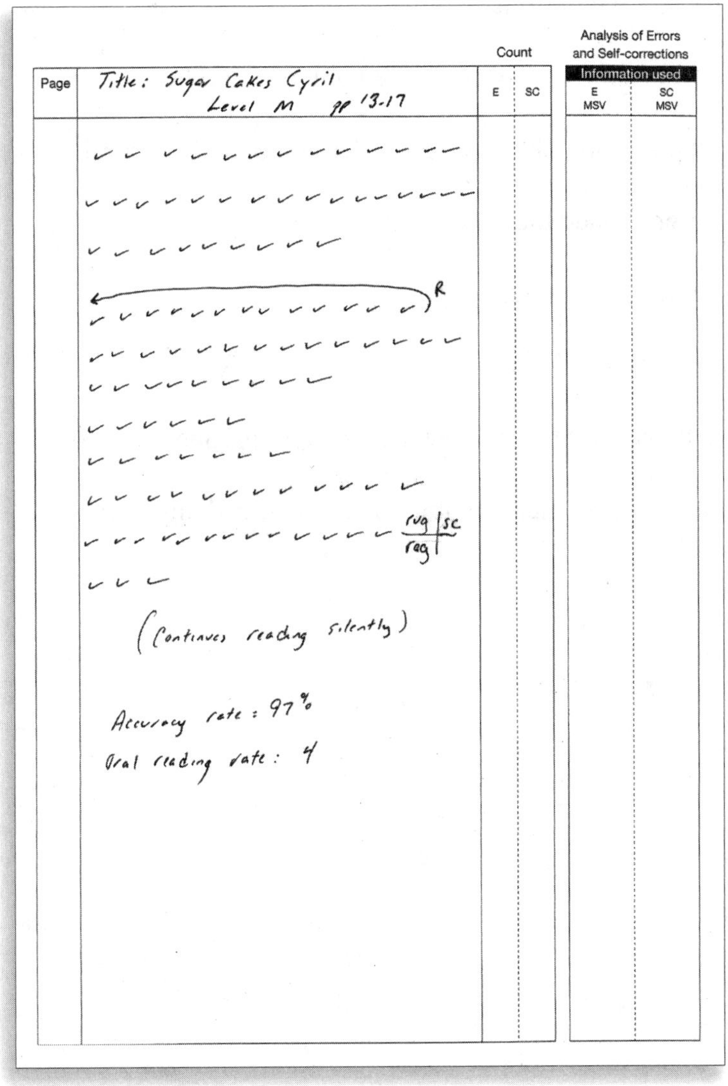
Count

Analysis of Errors and Self-corrections

Information used

Page

Title: Sugar Cakes Cyril

Level M pp 13-17

E | SC

E MSV | SC MSV

R

rug | sc

rag

(Continues reading silently)

Accuracy rate: 97%

Oral reading rate: 4

Figure A.1 A running record shows Emre's reading at level M. Use this to evaluate fluency, print work, and comprehension. The text excerpt has been provided on page 152 to help you evaluate errors and miscues within sentence context, and to allow you to properly evaluate his retelling and answers to comprehension questions (see page 153).

Running Record Sheet © 2005 by Marie M. Clay from *An Observation Survey of Early Literacy Achievement*, Third Edition (2013). Published by Global Education Systems Ltd. Reprinted by permission of the author's estate.

Sugar Cakes Cyril by Phillis Gershator

Since Cyril was the big brother, he was supposed to be the Big Helper. But it seemed like he was always in the way. If he poured the milk, it spilled. If he shut the door, it slammed.

And now, when he handed his mother the baby powder, he dropped it, and the top fell off. The powder spilled out onto the floor. It puffed up into the air and made them all cough.

"Go outside, Cyril," his mother snapped.

"I thought I was your Big Helper."

"I don't need a helper right now," she said, coughing. She finished diapering the baby and tried to clean up the powder with a damp rag. "Just go outside."

Summary

Cyril always wanted to be the helper, but Cyril's mom wanted him to go outside. He went outside. Then Ms. Elsie came, and put her heavy bags down. They brought the bags to the house. Cyril unlocked the food. Then Cyril cooked the food. Then Ms. Elsie tasted it.

Comp Qs

1. (Literal) How does Cyril make a mess?

   He kept dropping the baby powder.

2. (Literal) What does Cyril do to help Miss Elsie make the sugar cakes?

   He put the sugar in. He set oven to the correct temp. He added orange peels.

3. (Infer.) Why do you think Cyril says he hates the baby & his mommy?

   Because he has to help the baby and bring stuff to the baby. Too much work!

4. (Infer.) How do you think Cyril's feelings changed from the beginning to the end of the passage?

   He went from sad to happy. He was sad in the beginning because he wanted to help.

Whole-Book Assessment

Student Response Form

Student's name __Emre__   Grade __1__

Your teacher wants to learn more about you as a reader. For this reading activity, here are some simple steps to follow:

♦ Enjoy the book!

♦ When you reach a page with a sticky note, read to the bottom of the page.

♦ Stop and answer the question on your response form. Include as much detail as you can. It is fine to reread, but don't read ahead.

♦ Put the sticky note back in the book.

♦ Keep reading!

1. PAGE 7 What is a *baseball diamond*?

it's the basball feild

E (P) A I

2. PAGE 8 What is this page mostly about?

howmany players team butting feilding

E P (A) I

Figure A.2 A whole-book assessment from *Independent Reading Assessment: Nonfiction, Grade 3* (Serravallo 2013). (Note: When Emre tried to take the assessment at levels L and then K, his answers were mostly incorrect. This text, which is level J, shows that he has some areas of strength and some areas to work on.) To evaluate this assessment, see the expectations for readers in Figures 2.13–2.16. Note that the four strands' icons (a spotlight for "main idea," a key for "key details," a book and magnifying glass for "vocabulary," and a bar graph for "text features") on the escalating expectations graphics correspond to those on the left-hand margin of these pages, to help you evaluate the response by question type. A summary of the book *Play Ball* has also been provided for you on page 158.

Play Ball!
by Vanessa York

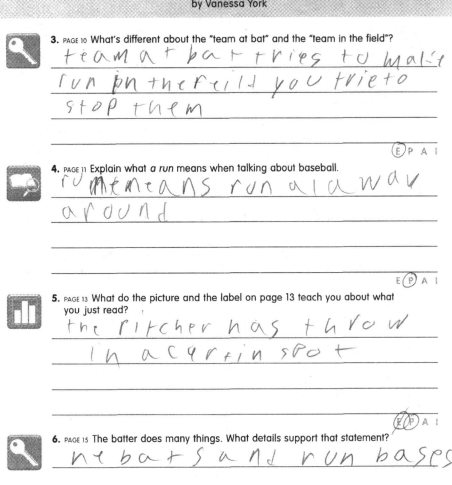

3. PAGE 10 What's different about the "team at bat" and the "team in the field"?

team at bat tries to make run on the feild you trie to stop them

E/(P) A I

4. PAGE 11 Explain what *a run* means when talking about baseball.

run memeans run ala way around

E (P) A I

5. PAGE 13 What do the picture and the label on page 13 teach you about what you just read?

the pitcher has throw in a cyrtin spot

(E/P) A I

6. PAGE 15 The batter does many things. What details support that statement?

ne bat s a nd run bases

E (P) A I

Independent Reading Assessment: Nonfiction © 2013 by Jennifer Serravallo • Scholastic Inc. **2**

7. PAGE 19 There are many ways to get an out. What details support that statement?

if he gets three strikes
hes out

E P (A) I

8. PAGE 24 What is the whole book mostly about?

barball

E P (A) I

Play Ball!
by Vanessa York

Reflection

Was this book easy, just right, or too hard? _just right_

How do you know? _because I cud read it easley_

Did you like this book? _yes_

Why or why not? _because I like basball_

Would you choose another book like this from the library? _yes_

Why or why not? _because I like books_

Play Ball! by Vanessa York

(Summary from *Independent Reading Assessment: Nonfiction, Grade 3,* Serravallo [2013])

When summer's on its way, what do kids like to do? Play baseball! This book explains how baseball works. In simple terms, with pictures and diagrams, it lays out the basic rules and the roles of the players.

Playing baseball

This section shows where baseball is played, who plays it, and how. A diagram on page 7 shows a baseball field, divided into the infield and the outfield. In the infield is the baseball diamond, made up of four bases: first base, second base, third base, and home plate.

There are two teams in a baseball game (page 8), and each game has nine innings. Each team gets a turn at bat and a turn in the field in every inning.

The team that scores the most runs wins (page 10). When a team is at bat, they try to score runs while the other team (in the field) tries to stop them. A run is when a player travels around the three bases and back to home plate, either in stages (stopping at each plate) or all at once. The player has to reach the bases before the ball does.

The Players

In this section, we learn about the job of the pitcher and the batter. The pitcher is the person who throws the ball. A good pitch has to reach a certain area in front of the batter's body called the "strike zone" (shown in a diagram on page 13). At the same time, the pitcher is trying to make the ball hard for the batter to hit.

The batter has to hit the ball, then run to first base before the ball gets there. If it's a good hit, the batter might be able to keep going—on to second base, third base, and maybe even back to home plate.

Strikes, Outs, and Home Runs

A strike is when a pitcher throws the ball into the strike zone but the batter swings and misses. If a batter has three strikes, he or she is out. A batter is also out if he or she hits the ball but one of the fielders catches it in the air. This is called a "fly ball." Or if the ball reaches a base before the batter gets there, the batter is out.

All batters want to hit home runs! This is when the ball flies far out into the outfield—or even out of the ballpark—and the batter makes it all the way around the bases without the fielders getting the ball there first.

Watching baseball

It's fun to watch baseball, either at home on TV, or at a stadium, cheering on your team. It's even more fun to go out and play!

Engagement Inventory

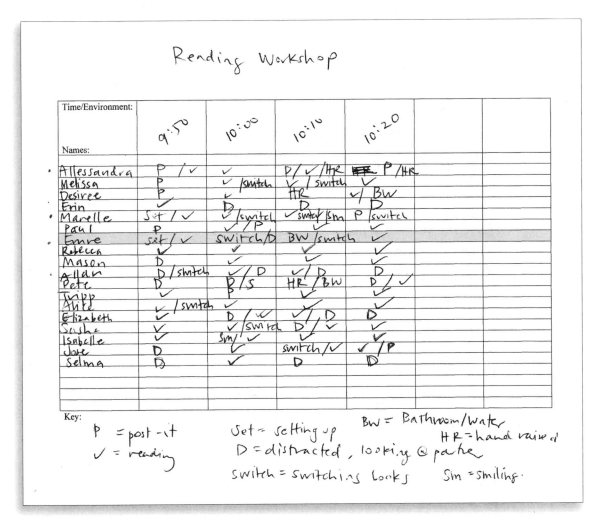

Figure A.3 An engagement inventory helps to give insight into Emre's focus, concentration, and motivation during one reader's workshop period.

Reading Interest Inventory

Emre

Feelings about reading?
Good. you get to discover new things, learn
new stuff. you get to see other stories
people made up to give you advice for your
stories.

Kinds?
Nonfiction, fiction
Hard books
Science books
sharks
Earth
Magic Tree House stories
Stink

Read to you?
No not really unless the books are really
really hard and I need help.

Where?
At home on the couch.

Read to?
(13)
My sister, mom, auntie.
Jeeps and Sheeps- something like that.

Figure A.4 A reading interest inventory in which Emre responded to five questions: What are your feelings about reading? What kinds of books do you like? Does anyone read to you at home? Where do you most like to read? Do you read to anyone? Use this to evaluate Emre's reading engagement.

Writing About Reading

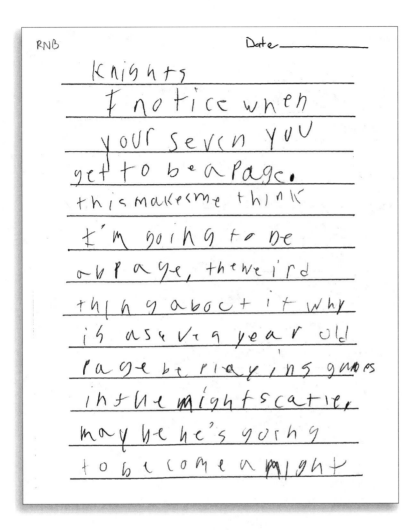

Figure A.5 A sample of writing about reading from Emre's reading notebook. Use this writing to evaluate Emre's comprehension.

(a translation of Emre's Reading Notebook entry with spelling and punctuation corrected)

Knights

I notice when you're seven you get to be a page. This makes me think I'm going to be a page. The weird thing about it why is a seven year old page be playing games in the knight's castle. Maybe he's going to become a knight.

Date_____

this makes me relize
pages love nights,
many perole dont
line wars but I think
wars are ausome,
on the other hand
I want to be in
the war to, this
All makes me think
that fighting
in wars is ausome,

This makes me realize pages love knights. Many people don't like wars but I think wars are awesome. On the other hand I want to be in the war too. This all makes me think that fighting in wars is awesome.

Narrative Writing

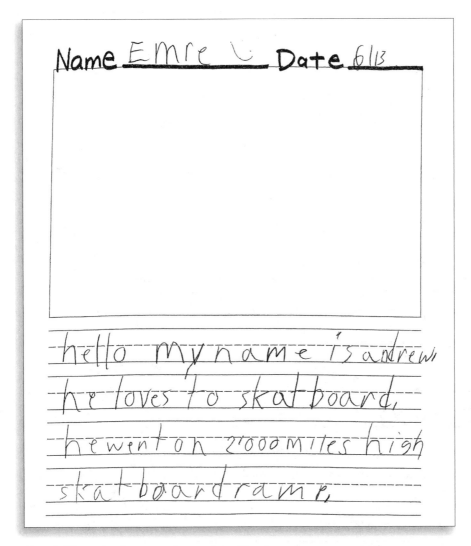

Emre's Narrative (punctuation and spelling have been corrected):

Hello. My name is Andrew. He loves to skateboard. He went on a 2,000 mile high skateboard ramp.

Figure A.6 A "finished" fictional story. Use this to evaluate qualities of narrative writing as well as his writing process.

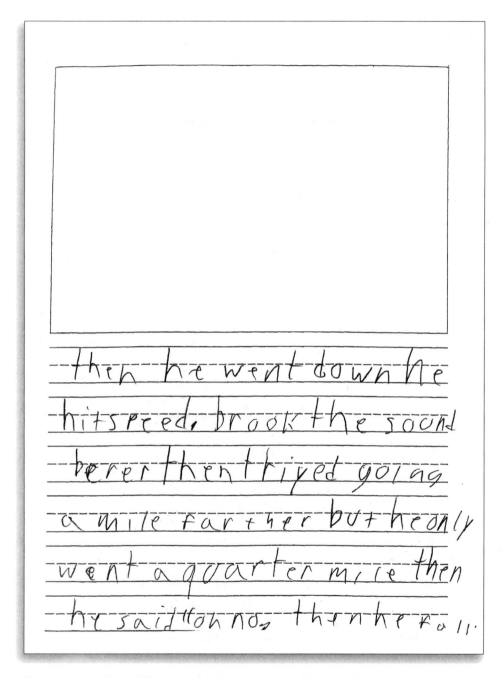

Then he went down. He hit speed, broke the sound barrier, then tried going a mile further but he only went a quarter mile then he said "Oh no!" then he fell.

e _____

too mph 200 mph 1000 mph

18'000 mph then he reached

200 hundred feet and

boom he smashed into the

ground and brook his leg.

100 mph, 200 mph, 1000 mph, 18,000 mph then he reached 200 feet and—boom!
He smashed into the ground and broke his leg.

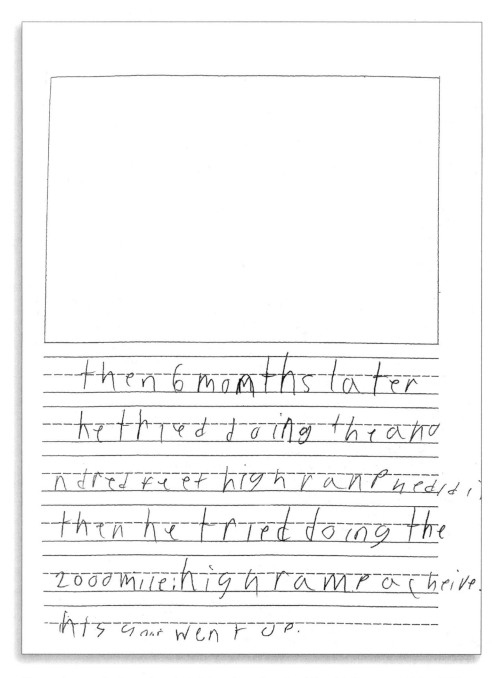

then 6 months later
he tried doing th a hu
ndred feet high ramP he did i
then he tried doing the
2000 mile high ramP acheive
his goal went up.

Then, six months later, he tried doing the a hundred feet high ramp and he did it.
Then he tried doing the 2,000 mile high ramp. He achieved his goal and went up.

Conversation Transcript

Allen: Will Miss Rue smile? This makes me think—

Emre: [interrupting] No! I go first, remember? [points at board] Allesandra goes first and I go second.

Allesandra: OK, whatever. Wait, let me go. I realize Miss Bruce is mean. I wonder why. This makes me think (inaudible)

Emre: [reading from sticky note] I wonder why the teacher is being so strict. Maybe she like Mrs. Fisher wants to learn more than usual [smiles].

Allesandra and boy: [giggle]

Allen: Is Miss Fisher really (inaudible).

Allessandra: Yeah, Miss Fisher is really (inaudible).

Allen: Will Miss Bruce Smile? [Emre closes his own book, talks to Allesandra and then looks away.] This makes me think (inaudible).

Allesandra: Wait! Guys, guys. What do you think?

Allen: It says it because right here she's trying to make Ms. Bruce laugh.

Emre: Ooh.

Allessandra: It does?

Allen: Yeah, it says it right here on the back.

Emre: Yeah it says it right here [lays down on his back on the floor, reading from back cover blurb]. Jake Drake Bully Buster, Jake Drake teacher's Pet. Wait, he's a pet?

Allesandra: [reads from back cover aloud simultaneously] Guys, why do you think? Why is she being mean to her own self?

Emre: [laying on floor, doing a backwards somersault] No, because she's a kid she's being mean.

Allessandra: I know! It's like a bully. Like a teacher bully.

Emre: A teenage bully.

Allen: My babysitter is a teenager.

Emre: I'm trying to make "teenage bully" a compound word.

Figure A.7 A shorthand transcript of Emre's conversation with his book club during reading workshop. Use this to analyze his conversational skills.

Step 2: Analyze Data

Compare my analysis of each example of Emre's work against your own analysis.

Tool	Strengths	Possibilities for Growth
Running record	• Reads accurately • Reads fluently (good phrasing and expression, appropriate word-per-minute rate) • Self-corrects for meaning (rug/rag) • Repeats to self-monitor • Recalls several events in sequence • Infers character feelings	• Recall the most important events (based on inference of what the story is really about) in sequence • Infer the meaning of words and phrases used figuratively (see question #3)
Whole-book assessment (independent reading assessment)	• Defines the meaning of content-specific vocabulary • Gives simple information about a text feature • Names the topic of a section or whole text • Supports an idea with one detail	• Give explanation of vocabulary • Connect the text feature to the main text • Determine a main idea by synthesizing multiple facts • Support an idea with many details

continues

Tool	Strengths	Possibilities for Growth
Engagement inventory	• Sets up to read quickly and starts reading	• Stamina—Emre seems to get distracted or want a break after about 5 minutes; he needs to begin by working toward 10 minutes before stopping • Stick with one book for the whole workshop—since he's reading longer chapter books, he shouldn't be switching between them after just 5–10 minutes
Reading interest inventory	• Has interest in a variety of types of books, both fiction and nonfiction • Asks for help when books are challenging • Has a place to read that works for him (couch)	• Work on changing concept of what's good about reading from reading "hard books" to reading more carefully in those books he does read • Encourage family participation in reading to and with him
Writing about reading (reading notebook)	• Retells a detail about the story • Reacts to the text ("awesome" and "weird")	• Explain the importance of an event to what's happening in the text • Connect events in the text • Convert reactions to fully formed ideas about the text

continues

Tool	Strengths	Possibilities for Growth
Narrative writing	• Structures story with a clear problem and solution • Includes one or two actions in each page/part • Uses dialogue once • Process—Fills the lines of the page	• Work on the connection between the problem and solution, so that the solution is more realistic • Use a variety of types of detail • Process—Use paper with more lines, and utilize the picture boxes to plan his writing
Conversation transcript	• Shares an idea (by reading from a sticky note) that relates to the topic of conversation • Wants to follow agreed upon rules for conversation • Reacts to the text and his club's ideas	• Elaborate more on his ideas (beyond just reading from a sticky note) • Elaborate on his reactions (more than just laughing)

Step 3: Interpret Data and Establish a Goal

INTERPRETATIONS

I think Emre needs to work on elaboration. In his reading, he gives brief answers to comprehension questions. In writing, his narrative shows only the most basic actions from a simple plot. When talking about his book, he just reads from his sticky note without added commentary. His responses to the whole-book assessment are very brief.

I think Emre needs to work on determining importance. In his reading, he mostly recalls literal facts from the story, although he is able to infer some character feelings. From his whole-book assessment, he recalls facts but doesn't think about the main idea. In his writing, he tends to write mostly action to the exclusion of other types of details.

I think Emre needs to work on inference and show, not tell. In his reading, he is just beginning to infer with his work around naming character feelings, but he could do more work to understand when something should have a literal versus figurative meaning. In his writing, he tells mostly just actions of the story, without showing character feelings or traits.

I think Emre needs to work on stamina in reading and writing. His writing feels almost rushed: he skips the pictures and goes right to writing words, and he writes very little considering the level at which he's able to read. The engagement inventory shows that he has a hard time staying focused for more than five to ten minutes at a time.

I think Emre needs to work on process. In writing, he seems to rush to get the words down and finish, without taking time to plan. In reading, he moves from book to book without a clear plan for his time, or an intention to read completely before starting another.

GOAL

Of these four, I am going to choose *determining importance*. I'm hoping that with a clearer focus and purpose for his reading and writing time, it will help correct some of the stamina and process issues. One of the strategies I can teach him might be to set about writing a story with a clear plan in mind, reading nonfiction to figure out what the author *really* wants us to know, and reading fiction thinking *what's a lesson I could learn from this story?* All of these will hopefully have a focusing effect on him and will also help him to think more deeply. Once he's spent some time thinking about the important ideas and themes in the books he reads and in the texts he writes, it'll then be time to turn to the other goals of elaboration, inferring, and showing not telling.

Step 4: Develop an Action Plan

STRATEGIES

- Reading (informational texts): Ask Emre to think about the *what* and the *so what*: What is the topic the author wants us to learn about? Have him list some of the facts that fit with the topic, and think "So what?": What's the point the author is trying to make about that topic?
- Reading (narrative): Ask Emre to concentrate on the *what* and the *why*: Think not just about what's happened, but why it might have happened. When he finds himself reacting to a spot in the text, have him record the *why* on a sticky note.
- Reading: See if moving him to a lower level gives him more opportunity to think with more depth.
- Reading: Introduce some prompts to his club that will get them talking and thinking about bigger ideas, such as: "What's this really about?" "What are we learning from this story/book/text?" "Why is this story/text important?" "What does the author want us to know about this topic/character?"
- Writing: Plan out a story by thinking first, "What do I want my story to be about?" Scaffold him in thinking about the answer to this question as not only about the topic of the story, but about the idea of the story.
- Writing: When writing informational texts, think about the topic and sub-topics. When he comes up with a topic, ask, "What do I think about this topic?" I expect he'll say things like the topic is "cool" or "weird," which is a fine start to getting him to decide which details to include, instead of including everything he knows.
- Writing: Utilize partnership time for his partner to ask him questions such as, "What are you trying to say?" and "What do you want your reader to know" and "What's important about this topic?"

METHODS

- Small-group strategy lessons: Introduce the strategies listed above in small groups with other students who need similar support.
- Conferences: Check in with Emre one-on-one when possible.
- Partnership: Offer prompts and questions to partners to help reinforce the work he's doing.

- Read aloud: Even though his classmates are reading at lower levels, occasionally plan some questions about big ideas in the text that the teacher reads aloud to the whole class.

TEACHING OVER TIME

- Try to see Emre in small group or conference once or twice a week in reading and once or twice in writing.
- Try to involve his family in reading with him and talking to him about a book's message (fiction) or main idea (nonfiction).

KNOWING WHEN THE GOAL HAS BEEN MET

- Reading: Look at Emre's stop-and-jots on sticky notes and in his notebook to see if he's talking about bigger ideas in the text. Listen in to conversation to see if he is more likely to talk about bigger ideas than an isolated event in the story. Or, when his group discusses an isolated event, note if they work to relate it back to the point of the text. Also, on his next running record he should be thinking more about the deeper meaning in the text.
- Writing: Emre has an improved process where he thinks and/or discusses what he wants to convey before beginning to write. When asked about his writing, he can tell you the point he was trying to make.

APPENDIX B
Glossary of Assessment Terms

In a data-driven educational climate, buzzwords abound. The days of getting by without hearing words like *formative, summative, universal screening,* and *progress monitoring* are in the past. We're all working to catch on quickly and make changes to our teaching practices so that we're aligned with the needs of today's classroom. Learning the meaning of these terms might help you assign language to some of what you already do and might help you identify areas that you've yet to explore. But the purpose of this book is to do more than just impress your friends at a dinner party with your edu-savvy vocabulary.

In this appendix, you'll learn some of the important aspects of assessment. Use the information to help you reflect on the assessments you use to get information about your readers and writers. See if there is a balance of the types of assessment you use and how you use them. If you discover there are types of assessments you aren't currently in the habit of using but would like to, I provide examples that are elaborated on in Chapter One.

Formative vs. Summative Assessment

Formative assessment is part of the instructional process. Formative assessments are collected and analyzed on the go and help teachers get information to both plan and modify instruction. Ideally, students are involved in reflecting on formative assessment. Teachers might help students by providing exemplars and/or benchmarks and guiding students in reflecting about their own work in comparison to the sample work.

Formative assessments are frequent and provide ongoing feedback to teachers and students about where students are in their learning journey. In this sense, formative assessment informs both teachers and students about student understanding at a point when timely adjustments can be made. Formative assessments typically aren't "graded."

Here are some examples of assessments that could be considered formative:

- book logs
- stop-and-jot writing in the midst of reading
- reading reflection
- on-demand writing sample

Summative assessments are given periodically to determine what students know and understand at a particular point in time. Sometimes summative assessments are given at the end of a unit of study or at predetermined time frames across the year. Many associate summative assessments only with standardized tests such as state assessments, but they can also be used to inform work within the classroom. Summative assessment at the district/classroom level is an accountability measure that is generally used as part of the grading process (Garrison, Chandler, and Ehringhaus 2009). Here are some examples of the types of assessments that could be considered summative assessments:

- state assessments
- district benchmark or interim assessments, such as running records (Directed Reading Assessment or the like)
- end-of-unit assessments
- published writing from an entire unit of study

Formal vs. Informal Assessments

Formal assessments are typically standardized. To be considered formal or standardized, they have been field-tested on students and have sometimes undergone some type of study by a scientist who studies testing, called a *psychometrician*. They have been deemed valid and reliable. *Valid* means that the assessment actually assesses what it says it does. *Reliable* means that if the same student were to take the same test more than once, the results would be comparable. The results of formal assessments are often reported as statistics, percentiles, or stanines—numbers. Some examples of formal assessments are:

- the Directed Reading Assessment
- state standardized tests
- college entrance exams such as the Scholastic Aptitude Test (SAT)
- IQ tests such as the Stanford-Binet

Informal assessments are often content and performance driven. Teachers may create tools to evaluate informal assessments, such as rubrics or checklists. Really any artifact that shows a student's learning or understanding could be considered an informal assessment. Results from an informal assessment are usually kept within the classroom and are not reported elsewhere. Examples of informal assessments may include:

- end-of-unit assessments
- a transcript of a student conversation

- an on-demand quick write in response to a prompt during a read-aloud
- a student's writing notebook sample

☐ Qualitative vs. Quantitative

Quantitative refers to numbers. Any type of assessment that yields a score, a number, a letter, or a percentage can be considered quantitative. Quantitative measures are erroneously what people typically think of when they use the word *data*. Often, quantitative data are valued over qualitative data by policy makers because it's easier to create graphs and charts, disaggregate the data, and perform statistical analyses on the data. However, for the purposes of guiding classroom instruction, it's important that a teacher has qualitative data as well. Quantitative data include:

- reading levels
- standardized test score
- reading rate (words/minute)

Qualitative measures attempt to provide descriptions of what is happening with the student, usually in words. Qualitative measures often allow teachers to be more nuanced and descriptive and offer more insight into not only the results, but also the why behind results. Examples include:

- a summary of the types of work a student has done over the course of a semester
- a student's written reflection on how he's accomplished his goal
- anecdotal records on a student's work during conferences

☐ Universal Screening

Universal screening takes place approximately three times across a school year. The purpose is to screen for, and identify, students whose reading achievement is significantly below what is expected so that a plan can be made for them to receive additional support. Universal screening has become particularly popular with the advent of Response to Intervention (RTI) initiatives.

If your school is deciding upon a universal screening tool, be aware that the best tools give a broad scope of "reading achievement." By contrast, tools such as Dynamic Indicators of Basic Early Literacy Skills (DIBELS) narrowly define what it means to read and don't offer helpful information about what to do once you've determined a child is in need of intervention (Goodman 2006; Pearson 2006). Universal screening tools that may more accurately reflect literacy practices you value and you're looking to support may include:

- *Benchmark Assessment System 1* (Fountas and Pinnell 2010)
- *Qualitative Reading Inventory—5* (Leslie and Caldwell 2010)
- *Analytical Reading Inventory* (Woods and Moe 2010)

ACTION →

Spread the student work examples you've collected, or Emre's, on the table in front of you. With a sticky note, use the terms in this section to label each artifact. Keep in mind that each artifact can fit into more than one category. For example, something can be both qualitative and formative.

☐ Progress Monitoring

Progress monitoring is a term used within an RTI framework that involves collecting repeated measures of performance to "(a) estimate rates of improvement, (b) identify students who are not demonstrating adequate progress, and/or (c) compare the efficacy of different forms of instruction to design more effective, individualized instruction" (National Center on Response to Intervention 2009).

Teachers can create their own tools or use tools available on the professional market (see www.rti4success.org or www.rtinetwork.org for more information). What's important is that any one type of assessment—say, oral reading rate—is not the only measure of performance considered. As already discussed, overreliance on one area of reading will give a warped perspective of the whole and may mislead a teacher to focus on an area of the child's reading that will not yield the desired progress (German and Newman 2007).

Forms   Reproducible forms are available to download at www.heinemann.com/products/E05300.aspx
(click on the Companion Resources tab).

Table for Summarizing Analysis of Data

Tool	Strengths	Possibilities for Growth
Reading Log	•	•
Writing about Reading	•	•
Running Record	•	•
Independent Reading Assessment	•	•

Possible Goals

I think _____ needs to _____

because I saw _____ when looking at the

_____, and _____

when looking at the _____.

I think _____ needs to _____

because I saw _____ when looking at the

_____, and _____

when looking at the _____.

I think _____ needs to _____

because I saw _____ when looking at the

_____, and _____

when looking at the _____.

I think _____ needs to _____

because I saw _____ when looking at the

_____, and _____

when looking at the _____.

Class Profile

Levels and Goals		
NAME	**LEVEL**	**GOAL AND NOTES**

Planning Your Week

	Monday	Tuesday	Wednesday	Thursday	Friday
Strategy Lesson (10 min)					
Strategy Lesson (10 min)					
Conferences (5 minutes each)					
Guided Reading (15–20 min)					
Other (_____ min)					
Notes					

Home–School Communication Letter

Dear _____,

_____ and I have recently had a conversation to set goals for the coming weeks of reading and writing. Goals help us to have a focus and intention when practicing reading and writing at home and at school. We wanted to let you know about our conversation so that you can provide support as well.

Reading Goal:	Writing Goal:

We expect that with daily practice, the goals will be accomplished on or around _____.

Here are some ways you can help _____ at home:

Reading	Writing

I welcome your thoughts and feedback!

Sincerely,

Note-Taking Form to Communicate with Other Teachers

Who	Date	Strengths	Teaching Possibilities

APPENDIX D

Possible Reading–Writing Correlations and Goals for Emergent Readers and Writers, and Students Reading at Levels A–F

Emergent Reading and Writing Correlations

The left-hand column is adapted from the work of Elizabeth Sulzby (1994). The right-hand column is based on my own observations of how writing development generally correlates to that of reading development in the emergent stages. Keep in mind that no child develops in lockstep, and writing abilities may surpass reading abilities and vice versa. This chart is not meant to be used as a checklist but instead as a general guideline to help teachers set meaningful goals within a child's zone of proximal development.

The shading in the chart represents meta-categories, or larger shifts, and numbers 1–11 indicate micro-categories.

Emergent Reading Categories *Behaviors and Skills*	Emergent Writing Categories *Behaviors and Skills*
1. Labels and comments on what's in the pictures	Draws pictures and when asked what's in the picture, will label and comment. "That's me, that's my mama."
2. Labels with actions	Draws pictures and when asked to tell what's in the picture includes action. "That's me and my mama going to the beach."
3. "Dialogic storytelling"—tells the story in dialogue, using pictures	Includes dialogue when telling a story from a picture she drew. "That's me and my mama at the beach when she said 'Look, a crab!' and then the crab went in the ocean."
4. "Monologic storytelling"—tells the story in narrative sequence, not dialogue	Includes a narrative sequence when telling a picture, possibly within one picture (pointing to parts) or across pages

continues

Emergent Reading and Writing (cont.)

Emergent Reading Categories *Behaviors and Skills*	Emergent Writing Categories *Behaviors and Skills*
5. Reads using pictures with a mix of oral storytelling and story language	Elaborates when telling a story from a picture, including many details and/or sentences per picture
6. Reads using story language with little elaboration, relying on pictures	"Writes" a story across pages (using pictures). When telling back the story, will link one page to the next with transitional words and/or phrases.
7. Sounds like the child is reading the story with elaboration, but she is really using the pictures	"Writes" a story across pages (using pictures). When telling back the story, will sound like embellished storytelling with action, dialogue, and or descriptions of setting or characters.
8. Refuses to read because he realizes that he needs the print to read the story ("I can't read this book. I don't know those words.")	Starts to spend time writing print on the page—labeling pictures, writing a string of letters, and/or an attempting a sentence on the bottom of the page
9. Reads text connecting all the pages together and identifies some letters and words. It sounds just like stage 7, but the child may add, "Look, there's a c" or "Look, that word is and."	Writes some recognizable words, such as high-frequency words, words copied from around the classroom, and/or names the child knows how to spell. The child is able to use invented spelling when writing. When reading back his writing, the child sounds like stage 7, but may also point to some of the labels next to pictures and/or some of the words in the sentence(s) below the picture.
10. Reads with expression and connects all the parts of the story together. The child may be running a finger under the words, but isn't one-to-one matching.	The student is likely to attempt a sentence written on the line(s). When telling the story, the child may be running a finger under the lines, although the actually telling of the story may elaborate beyond what's written.
11. Cross-checks the reading of the story with some print on the page and revises when needed using meaning, pictures, story language, and print. The child attends to some of the print, matching one-to-one while reading.	The child has written a sentence with spaces between words, and words have beginning and ending sounds (and perhaps some medial sounds). When reading back his writing, the child follows the written words on the page more closely, often if not always matching one-to-one.

Levels A and B Reading and Writing Correlations

Reading Behaviors/Skills	Writing Behaviors/Skills
Decoding and Encoding, Strengthening Concept of Word vs. Letter	
• Tracks print with finger (working on 1:1 match)	• Writes at least 2–5 labels with beginning sounds
	• Writes random letter strings at bottom of page and reads back with finger
	• Reads back labels with 1:1 match
	• Writes a sentence with spaces between words
• Recognizes some known sight words often	• Writes known sight words often
Strengthening Reading and Writing Behaviors, and Concepts of Print	
• Moves from left to right when reading (within one page and across pages)	• Labels words using letters in left to right order
	• "Reads" random letter strings with finger from left to right
	• Writes pages of a book in left to right order
Strengthening Meaning Cueing System	
• Uses the illustrations in the story as a source of information	• Uses the pictures to remember and reread writing
	• "Writes" a story using pictures to represent characters, place, and some action
Volume	
• Reads 10–12 books a week, most of them reread three or more times	• Draws a picture with labels
	• Writes several 1-page pieces per day or writes one 2- or 3-page booklet per day

Since there is such a wide variation across grades and across levels, these tables can be used to gain a sense of general behaviors by stage and/or level and how expectations for reading and writing might connect and shift and change based on level. Of course, children's reading and writing growth doesn't develop in lockstep, and these tables are meant to be used as general guidelines, not checklists. The tables on these pages rely heavily on the work in Fountas and Pinnell's *Continuum of Literacy Learning* (2010).

Levels C and D Reading and Writing Correlations

Reading Behaviors/Skills	Writing Behaviors/Skills
Working with Print: Encoding/Decoding	
• Uses some of the letter(s) of a word, including some of the final letters to figure out unknown words	• Spells words with beginning and ending consonant sounds • Progresses to spelling words with medial consonant sounds and logical vowel substitutions
• Makes return sweep on more than one line of print	• Writes 1–4 lines of print/sentences per page in the correct direction (left to right) and returning on the next line
• Reads known words in text automatically	• Spells some known words correctly
Integrating The Three Cueing Systems: Meaning, Syntax, Visual	
• Begins to integrate sources of information (meaning, syntax, visual) • Cross-checks to make sure the reading looks right, sounds right, and makes sense	• Reads back writing with 1:1 match • Uses pictures and letters as sources of information • Rereads and revises to make sure the writing makes sense, sounds right, looks right
Volume	
• Reads 10–12 books a week, most of them reread three or more times	• Writes 1 or more sentence on a page • Writes one 2-3 page booklet every other day
Comprehension/Structure and Elaboration	
• Retells a story in one to two sentences • Can infer a character's feeling • Relies on pictures for meaning.	• Writes stories with a beginning and end (and maybe a middle) • Shows character feeling in drawings (and maybe in labels)

Since there is such a wide variation across grades and across levels, these tables can be used to gain a sense of general behaviors by stage and/or level and how expectations for reading and writing might connect and shift and change based on level. Of course, children's reading and writing growth doesn't develop in lockstep, and these tables are meant to be used as general guidelines, not checklists. The tables on these pages rely heavily on the work in Fountas and Pinnell's *Continuum of Literacy Learning* (2010).

Levels E and F Reading and Writing Correlations

Reading Behaviors/Skills	Writing Behaviors/Skills
Figuring Out Print—Decoding/Encoding	
• Uses internal parts of words along with beginnings and endings (including blends and digraphs) • Becomes aware of inflectional endings (-s, -ing, -ed) and works to read them correctly	• Spells words letter by word part • Spells most short vowels correctly • Starts to use and sometimes confuse blends and digraphs • Begins to spell with inflectional endings (-s, -ing, -ed) • Rereads to make sure their work "looks right"
Focusing on Making Meaning	
• Thinks about what's happening in the story to figure out an unknown word • Uses pictures to figure out unknown words • Uses prior knowledge to figure out unknown words	• Uses reading strategies in his own writing. For example, when a child can't reread his writing but he uses the meaning (and picture) to help him figure out what he meant to write • Uses pictures to help him write, by looking at his picture and adding more words • Rereads and edits work to make sure his work "makes sense"
Figuring Out Print—Supporting Syntactical Cueing Systems/Writing Grammatically Correctly	
• Reads and understands compound sentences • Reads a variety of sentence structures, including those that begin with subjects, or adjectives, or verbs	• Writes with a variety of sentence structures, including simple and compound sentences • Rereads and edits work to make sure his sentences "sound right"
Cross-Checking and Revising (Process)	
• Cross-checks multiple sources of information • Rereads books to think more about the story • Reads to partners	• Rereads to add on or self-correct • Rereads writing to add on/delete • Rereads to share with an audience

continues

Since there is such a wide variation across grades and across levels, these tables can be used to gain a sense of general behaviors by stage and/or level and how expectations for reading and writing might connect and shift and change based on level. Of course, children's reading and writing growth doesn't develop in lockstep, and these tables are meant to be used as general guidelines, not checklists. The tables on these pages rely heavily on the work in Fountas and Pinnell's *Continuum of Literacy Learning* (2010).

Levels E and F Reading and Writing Correlations (cont.)

Reading Behaviors/Skills	Writing Behaviors/Skills
Volume	
• Reads 10–12 books a week, most of them reread three or more times	• Writes 1–2 sentences on a page • Writes one 3- to 5-page booklet every other day
Comprehension/Elaboration and Structure	
• Retells with problem/solution *or* with pattern/change across the story including a few main events • Recognizes who characters are and where the story takes place • Understands that story endings communicate a subtle meaning that must be interpreted from the story	• Writes with story structure including a problem and solution. The story has a few main events. Each action/step is told in 1 or 2 sentences • Writes stories with characters and setting • Writes pieces with a sense of ending • Thinks about a bigger meaning his story has • Considers audience, and may match some details in consideration of the audience • Focuses on one topic/small moment • Attempts elaboration that matches meaning
Fluency	
• Begins to demonstrate appropriate stress on words (changes voice for punctuation) • In repeated reads, begins to read with 2- and 3- word phrases • Reads known words automatically • Reads texts with increasingly more lines of print per page	• Approximates end punctuation in simple sentences • Knows how to do his best and keep going • Spells sight words quickly and automatically • Rereads own writing with expression

Since there is such a wide variation across grades and across levels, these tables can be used to gain a sense of general behaviors by stage and/or level and how expectations for reading and writing might connect and shift and change based on level. Of course, children's reading and writing growth doesn't develop in lockstep, and these tables are meant to be used as general guidelines, not checklists. The tables on these pages rely heavily on the work in Fountas and Pinnell's *Continuum of Literacy Learning* (2010).

Works Cited

Adler, David A. Various dates. Cam Jansen series. New York, NY: Puffin.

Afflerbach, Peter, P. David Pearson, and Scott G. Paris. 2008. "Clarifying Differences Between Reading Skills and Reading Strategies." *The Reading Teacher* 61 (5): 364–373.

Allington, Richard L. 2011. *What Really Matters for Struggling Readers: Designing Research-Based Programs.* 3d ed. New York, NY: Pearson.

Anderson, Carl. 2000. *How's It Going? A Practical Guide to Conferring with Student Writers.* Portsmouth, NH: Heinemann.

———. 2005. *Assessing Writers.* Portsmouth, NH: Heinemann.

Arnold, Tedd. Various dates. Fly Guy series. New York, NY: Scholastic.

Bear, Donald R., Marcia R. Invernizzi, Shane Templeton, and Francine R. Johnston. 2011. *Words Their Way: Word Study for Phonics, Vocabulary, and Spelling Instruction.* 5th ed. New York, NY: Pearson.

Beaver, Joetta M. 2006. *Development Reading Assessment, K–3.* 2nd ed. Parsippany, NJ: Pearson.

Boelts, Maribeth. 2009. *Those Shoes.* Somerville, MA: Candlewick Press.

Bomer, Randy, and Katherine Bomer. 2001. *For a Better World: Reading and Writing for Social Action.* Portsmouth, NH: Heinemann.

Calkins, Lucy McCormick. 2000. *The Art of Teaching Reading.* New York, NY: Pearson.

Calkins, Lucy, Amanda Hartman, and Zoe Ryder White. 2005. *One to One: The Art of Conferring with Young Writers.* Portsmouth, NH: Heinemann.

Calkins, Lucy, with Colleagues from the Reading and Writing Project. 2011. *Curricular Plans for the Reading and Writing Workshop, Grades K–8.* Portsmouth, NH: Heinemann.

———. 2013. *Units of Study in Opinion, Information, and Narrative Writing: A Common Core Workshop Curriculum.* Portsmouth, NH: Heinemann.

Clay, Marie. 1991. *Becoming Literate.* Portsmouth, NH: Heinemann.

———. 2000. *Running Records for Classroom Teachers.* Portsmouth, NH: Heinemann.

———. 2013. *An Observation Survey of Early Literacy Achievement.* Portsmouth, NH: Heinemann.

Collins, Kathy. 2004. *Growing Readers: Units of Study in the Primary Classroom.* Portland, ME: Stenhouse Publishers.

———. 2008. *Reading for Real: Teach Students to Read with Power, Intention, and Joy in K–3 Classrooms.* Portland, ME: Stenhouse Publishers.

Cruz, M. Colleen. 2004. *Independent Writing: One Teacher—Thirty-Two Needs, Topics, and Plans.* Portsmouth, NH: Heinemann.

Cunningham, Patricia M., and Richard L. Allington. 2010. *Classrooms That Work: They Can All Read and Write.* 5th ed. New York, NY: Pearson.

Danziger, Paula. Varous dates. Amber Brown series. New York, NY: Puffin.

Daunis, Sarah and Maria C. Iams. 2007. *Text Savvy: Using a Shared Reading Framework to Build Comprehension, Grades 3–6.* Portsmouth, NH: Heinemann.

Duffy, G. G., et al. 1987. "Effects of Explaining the Reasoning Associated with Using Reading Strategies." *Reading Research Quarterly* 22: 347–368.

Ericsson, K. Anders, Ralf Th. Krampe, and Clemens Tesch-Römer. 1993. "The Role of Deliberate Practice in the Acquisition of Expert Performance." *Psychological Review* 100 (3): 363–406.

Fisher, Douglas, and Nancy Frey. 2008. *Better Learning Through Structured Teaching: A Framework for the Gradual Release of Responsibility.* Alexandria, VA: Association for Supervision and Curriculum Development.

Fisher, Douglas, Nancy Frey, and Diane Lapp. 2012. *Text Complexity: Raising Rigor in Reading.* Newark, DE: International Reading Association.

Fountas, Irene C., and Gay Su Pinnell. 1996. *Guided Reading: Good First Teaching for All Children.* Portsmouth, NH: Heinemann.

———. 1998. *Word Matters: Teaching Phonics and Spelling in the Reading/Writing Classroom.* Portsmouth, NH: Heinemann.

———. 2006. *Teaching for Comprehending and Fluency. Thinking, Talking, and Writing About Reading, K–8.* Portsmouth, NH: Heinemann.

———. 2008. *Leveled Literacy Intervention* (Blue System). Portsmouth, NH: Heinemann.

———. 2009. *When Readers Struggle: Teaching That Works.* Portsmouth, NH: Heinemann.

———. 2010. *The Continuum of Literacy Learning, Grades PreK–8,* 2d ed. Portsmouth, NH: Heinemann.

———. 2010. *Benchmark Assessment System 1*, 2d ed. Portsmouth, NH: Heinemann.

Freeman, Don. 1976. *Corduroy.* New York, NY: Puffin

Garrison, Catherine, Dennis Chandler, and Michael Ehringhaus. 2009. *Effective Classroom Assessment: Linking Assessment with Instruction.* Westerville, OH: Association for Middle Level Education.

German, Diane J., and Rochelle S. Newman. 2007. "Oral Reading Skills of Children with Oral Language (Word-Finding) Difficulties." *Reading Psychology* 28 (5): 397–442.

Gladwell, Malcolm. 2002. *The Tipping Point: How Little Things Can Make a Big Difference.* New York, NY: Back Bay Books.

Goodman, Kenneth S. 2006. "A Critical Review of DIBELS." In *The Truth About DIBELS: What It Is—What It Does,* ed. Kenneth S. Goodman, 1–39. Portsmouth, NH: Heinemann.

Guthrie, John T., and Allan Wigfield. 1997. *Reading Engagement: Motivating Readers Through Integrated Instruction. Newark, DE: International Reading Association.*

Harris, Albert J., and Edward R. Sipay. 1990. *How to Increase Reading Ability: A Guide to Developmental and Remedial Methods.* London, England: Longman Publishing Group.

Harvey, Stephanie, and Anne Goudvis. 2007. *Strategies That Work: Teaching Comprehension for Understanding and Engagement.* 2d ed. Portland, ME: Stenhouse Publishers.

Hattie, John. 1999. "Influences on Student Learning." Available from http://www
.education.auckland.ac.nz/webdav/site/education/shared/hattie/docs/influences-on-
student-learning.pdf. Last accessed October 17, 2013.

Holdaway, Donald. 1984. *The Foundations of Literacy.* Portsmouth, NH: Heinemann.

Johnston, Peter H. 2004. *Choice Words: How Our Language Affects Children's Learning.* Portland, ME: Stenhouse Publishers.

Keene, Ellin Oliver. 2006. *Assessing Comprehension Thinking Strategies.* Huntington Beach, CA: Shell Education.

Keene, Ellin Oliver, and Susan Zimmermann. 2007. *Mosaic of Thought: The Power of Comprehension Strategy Instruction,* 2d ed. Portsmouth, NH: Heinemann.

Keene, Ellin Oliver, et al. 2011. *Comprehension Going Forward: Where We Are / What's Next.* Portsmouth, NH: Heinemann.

Koch, Richard. 2008. *The 80/20 Principle: The Secret of Achieving More with Less.* 2d ed. New York, NY: Doubleday.

Kuhn, Melanie R. 2008. *The Hows and Whys of Fluency Instruction.* New York, NY: Pearson.

Leslie, Lauren, and JoAnne Schudt Caldwell. 2010. *Qualitative Reading Inventory—5.* Upper Saddle River, NJ: Pearson.

Martinelli, Marjorie, and Kristi Mraz. 2012. *Smarter Charts K–2: Optimizing and Instructional Staple to Create Independent Readers and Writers.* Portsmouth, NH: Heinemann.

McCarrier, Andrea, Gay Su Pinnell, and Irene C. Fountas. 1999. *Interactive Writing: How Language & Literacy Come Together, K–2.* Portsmouth, NH: Heinemann.

McGill-Franzen, Anne. 2006. *Kindergarten Literacy: Matching Assessment and Instruction in Kindergarten.* New York, NY: Scholastic Inc.

Mermelstein, Leah. 2013. *Self-Directed Writers: The Third Essential Element in the Writing Workshop.* Portsmouth, NH: Heinemann.

Miller, Debbie. 2013. *Reading with Meaning: Teaching Comprehension in the Primary Grades*, 2d ed. Portland, ME: Stenhouse Publishers.

National Center on Response to Intervention. 2009. Available from http://www.rti4success.org/categorycontents/progress_monitoring. Last accessed October 17, 2013.

National Governors Association Center for Best Practices and Council of Chief State School Officers. 2010. Common Core State Standards. Available from http://www.corestandards.org. Last accessed October 17, 2013.

Nichols, Maria. 2006. *Comprehension Through Conversation: The Power of Purposeful Talk in the Reading Workshop.* Portsmouth, NH: Heinemann.

Paris, Scott. G., David R. Cross, and Marjorie Y. Lipson. 1984. "Informed Strategies for Learning: A Program to Improve Children's Reading Awareness and Comprehension." *Journal of Educational Psychology* 76: 1239–1252.

Parkes, Brenda. 2000. *Read It Again! Revisiting Shared Reading.* Portland, ME: Stenhouse Publishers.

Parsons, Stephanie. 2005. *First Grade Writers: Units of Study to Help Children Plan, Organize, and Structure Their Ideas.* Portsmouth, NH: Heinemann.

———. 2007. *Second Grade Writers: Units of Study to Help Children Focus on Audience and Purpose*. Portsmouth, NH: Heinemann.

———. 2010. *First Grade Readers: Units of Study to Help Children See Themselves as Meaning Makers*. Portsmouth, NH: Heinemann.

Pearson, P. David. 2006. Foreword to *The Truth About DIBELS*, ed. Kenneth S. Goodman, v–xxiv. Portsmouth, NH: Heinemann.

Pearson, P. David, and Margaret C. Gallagher. 1983. "The Instruction of Reading Comprehension." *Contemporary Educational Psychology* (8): 317–344.

Pearson, P. David, Laura R. Roehler, Janice A. Dole, and Gerald G. Duffy. 1992. "Developing Expertise in Reading Comprehension." In *What Research Has to Say About Reading Instruction*. 2d ed. Eds. S. Jay Samuels and Alan E. Farstrup, 145–199. Newark, DE: International Reading Association.

Petty, Geoffrey. 2006. *Evidence Based Teaching: A Practical Approach*. Cheltenham, UK: Nelson Thornes.

Pink, Daniel H. 2011. *Drive: The Surprising Truth About What Motivates Us*. New ed. New York, NY: Riverhead Books.

Rasinski, Timothy. 2010. *The Fluent Reader: Oral & Silent Reading Strategies for Building Fluency, Word Recognition & Comprehension*. 2d ed. New York, NY: Scholastic.

Ray, Katie Wood. 2010. *In Pictures and In Words: Teaching the Qualities of Good Writing Through Illustration Study*. Portsmouth, NH: Heinemann.

Ray, Katie Wood, and Matt Glover. 2008. *Already Ready: Nurturing Writers in Preschool and Kindergarten*. Portsmouth, NH: Heinemann.

Routman, Regie. 1994. *Invitations: Changing as Teachers and Learners K–12*. Portsmouth, NH: Heinemann.

Serravallo, Jennifer. 2010. *Teaching Reading in Small Groups: Differentiated Instruction for Building Strategic, Independent Readers*. Portsmouth, NH: Heinemann.

———. 2012. *Independent Reading Assessment: Fiction, Grade 3*. New York, NY: Scholastic.

———. 2012. *Independent Reading Assessment: Fiction, Grade 4*. New York, NY: Scholastic.

———. 2012. *Independent Reading Assessment: Fiction, Grade 5*. New York, NY: Scholastic.

———. 2013. *Independent Reading Assessment: Nonfiction, Grade 3*. New York, NY: Scholastic.

———. 2013. *Independent Reading Assessment: Nonfiction, Grade 4*. New York, NY: Scholastic.

———. 2013. *Independent Reading Assessment: Nonfiction, Grade 5*. New York, NY: Scholastic.

———. 2014. *The Literacy Teacher's Playbook, Grades 3–6: Four Steps for Turning Assessment Data into Goal-Directed Instruction*. Portsmouth, NH: Heinemann.

Serravallo, Jen, and Gravity Goldberg. 2007. *Conferring with Readers: Supporting Each Student's Growth and Independence*. Portsmouth, NH: Heinemann.

Shannon, David. 1998. *No, David!* Blue Sky Press. New York, NY: Scholastic.

Shaw, Nancy E. 1997. *Sheep in a Jeep*. Boston, MA: Houghton Mifflin Harcourt.

Slobodkina, Esphyr. 1968. *Caps for Sale*. New York, NY: HarperCollins.

Spinelli, Jerry. 1999. *Maniac McGee*. New York, NY: Little, Brown, and Company.

Sulzby, Elizabeth. 1994. Children's Emergent Reading of Favorite Storybooks. In *Theoretical Models and Processes of Reading*. 4th ed. Eds. R. B. Ruddell, M. R. Ruddell, and H. Singer, 244–280. Newark, DE: International Reading Association.

Taberski, Sharon. 2000. *On Solid Ground: Strategies for Teaching Reading, K–3*. Portsmouth, NH: Heinemann.

———. 2010. *Comprehension from the Ground Up: Simplified, Sensible Instruction for the K–3 Reading Workshop*. Portsmouth, NH: Heinemann.

Truss, Lynne. 2006. *Eats, Shoots & Leaves: The Zero Tolerance Approach to Punctuation*. New York, NY: Gotham Books.

Vygotsky, Lev. 1978. "Interaction Between Learning and Development." In *Mind in Society: The Development of Higher Psychological Processes*. Cambridge, MA: Harvard University Press.

Wiggins, Grant. 2013. "On So-Called 'Reading Strategies'—The Utter Mess That Is the Literature and Advice to Teachers." Available from http://grantwiggins.wordpress.com/2013/03/04/on-so-called-reading-strategies-the-utter-mess-that-is-the-literature-and-advice-to-teachers/. Last accessed June 19, 2013.

Wood, David, Jerome S. Bruner, and Gail Ross. 1976. "The Role of Tutoring in Problem Solving." *Journal of Child Psychology and Psychiatry* 17 (2): 89–100.

Woods, Mary Lynn, and Alden J. Moe. 2010. *Analytical Reading Inventory: Comprehensive Standards-Based Assessment for all Students Including Gifted and Remedial*. 9th ed. New York, NY: Pearson.

York, Vanessa. *Play Ball*. New York, NY: Scholastic.

Zimmermann, Susan, and Chryse Hutchins. 2003. *7 Keys to Comprehension: How to Help Your Kids Read It and Get It!* New York, NY: Three Rivers Press.

Zion, Gene. 2006. *Harry the Dirty Dog*. New York, NY: HarperCollins.